just say nu

just say nu

YIDDISH FOR EVERY OCCASION
(WHEN ENGLISH JUST WON'T DO)

Michael Wex

ST. MARTIN'S PRESS

NEW YORK

www.stmartins.com

Library of Congress Cataloging-in-Publication Data

Wex, Michael, 1954–
    Just say nu : Yiddish for every occasion (when English just won't do)
        p.   cm.
    Includes bibliographical references and index.
    ISBN-13: 978-0-312-36462-5
    ISBN-10: 0-312-36462-8
    1. Yiddish language—Terms and phrases.   2. Yiddish language—Social aspects.   3. Yiddish language—Idioms.   4. Proverbs, Yiddish.   5. Yiddish wit and humor.   I. Title.

PJ5113.W485 2007
439'.181—dc22

                                                        2007019667

First Edition: October 2007

10   9   8   7   6   5   4   3   2   1

For Rill,
with love

contents

Contents

acknowledgments

This book owes its existence, along with much of its contents, to people whom I have yet to meet: readers of *Born to Kvetch* who e-mailed me with questions about Yiddish idioms and ways of speech not covered (or not covered in enough detail for them) in that book. Much of what follows are answers to those questions.

One reader, Cliff Gevirtz, thought it would be a good idea if I were to put together a guide for people who'd like to use a bit of Yiddish in their day-to-day lives. Alison Lazarus passed his suggestion along to Ethan Friedman, who passed it on to me. I owe Ethan a tremendous debt of gratitude for his editorial work on this volume; his enthusiasm and understanding are apparent on every page.

George Witte stepped in at a crucial moment and made sure that this project came to fruition.

This book could not have seen the light of day without Nichole Argyres, who succeeded Ethan at St. Martin's. Kylah McNeill took care of many of the details. I'd also like to thank Stefanie Lindskog.

My agent, Gareth Esersky, was instrumental in the development of this project, which has kept her plenty busy since it started. Carol Mann's help has also been invaluable.

My wife, Marilla, managed to endure months on end of hearing little, if any, English at home, while Sabina, my daughter, remains an endless source of love and delight, one that grows taller with each passing day.

just say nu

introduction

What It's All About

PICTURE me ten years ago, desperate and broke. I'm in an editing suite, watching porn with a producer. "So you see what's happening here?" he asks. "She's switched rooms with the rabbi's wife, but the desk clerk forgot to tell the rabbi. When he comes back at night, he goes straight to the room and jumps into bed. . . . He's gotta *say* something, know what I mean? Think you can do it?"

I'd spent my life getting ready for it: A non-Jew was going to give me money to say four or five words in Yiddish. I nodded, he set some levels, and off we went. *"Oy,"* I moaned, watching the rabbi's face on the screen, *"Oy, Shprintse"*—I'd given the rabbi's wife a good old-fashioned Yiddish name—*"Oy! Oy! Shprintse,"* the rabbi was about to climax. *"Oy-vay-iz-meer-Shprintse . . . Oy vay."*

"Oy vay?" The producer was yelling into my headphones. *"Oy vay?* Don't think you can screw with me just because I'm not Jewish. Now let's do it again and let's do it right. Tell me what you say when you come."

I'd just told him, but he didn't want to know. The rest was all his fault. *"Nu,"* I said. "What you really say is *nu."*

"Then say it. And don't say anything else. Just say *nu."*

There's something almost Zen-like about it, the idea that the same set of words and expressions can be used to express pain and pleasure, joy and sorrow, satisfaction and discontent. Since none of it is going to last, why bother to name *two* sets of phantoms, as if the cosmos were a kosher kitchen and illusions could be dairy or meat? If all life is suffering, then *oy vay iz meer*—"o, woe is me"—is the proper response to everything.

Most Jews are not Buddhists, though, let alone students of Zen. While virtually any Yiddish-speaker would subscribe to the first of the Buddha's Four Noble Truths—the idea that to live is to suffer—he or she would probably differ with the Buddha on the final cause of that suffering. It isn't desire that gets in the way of happiness; the Jews' problems are rooted in devotion to the immutable rather than attachment to transitory things or ideas:

MEH KEN LAIBM

You could live,

as they say in Yiddish. The problem is not even vaguely metaphysical. Life in the fullest sense of the word is indeed possible in this sublunary, material world; life is what it's here for.

MEH KEN LAIBM

You could live,

as any Yiddish-speaking Jew can tell you,

Ober MEH LOZT NISHT

but they won't let you.

It isn't life that's to blame, it's the living. Just about all of them. There are a lot of them, they're all out to get you—and worse, as far as *they're* concerned, it's *your* fault.

Yiddish is under no illusions about the nobility of human nature; the language and its approach to life owe their existence to the destruction of Jerusalem and the Temple, to the exile of the whole of the Jewish people. And what caused all of this to happen? What started a chain of generally unpleasant events that is still unfolding? What momentous occurrence brought it all about?

A man was thrown out of a party to which he'd been invited by mistake.*

Yiddish offers a refreshingly realistic view of human life and motivation. While it is unfair to say that Yiddish glories in human small-mindedness, Yiddish is certainly not afraid to acknowledge the importance of small-mindedness in human affairs. In the Yiddish world, where sages and tradesmen were often the very same people, happiness, contentment of the most inconsequential sort, is like a wallet full of cash: great to have, dumb to flash.

Pleasure thus tends to be taken quietly, in private. It isn't that Yiddish-speakers are never happy; they're happy, all right, they just don't want to admit it. They're wary of having others come in and rain on their parade—whether those others are human beings or the wicked spirits and evil eyes that are believed to bedevil all humanity. Best keep your happiness inside, where it's less likely to be stolen or disturbed. As the Bible tells us, "And Judah and Israel dwelt in safety, each man under his vine and each under his fig tree" (I Kings 5:5, in the Hebrew). A *mentsh,* a decent and proper human being, doesn't have to be satisfied with his or her own vine or fig tree; a *mentsh* merely makes sure that his or her vine or fig tree isn't enlarged at the expense of someone else's.

It is difficult to divorce these ethical and superstitious currents from the historical conditions that led to the development of a mentality that holds the real value of an education to be that "they can never take it away from you"—as if gangs of ravening goyim were going to launch an academic search-and-seizure pogrom to plunder your memories of Statistics 101. Yiddish-speaking Jews are the teenagers among the peoples of the world, afraid to say that they like anything lest it, too, be taken away from them by their

---

* See Babylonian Talmud, Tractate Gitin, folio 55b.

stern, often angry father or the juvenile delinquent babysitters into whose hands He has cast them.

This is the feeling that leads to the famous old joke about two Jews who meet after not having seen each other for some time. *"Nu?"* says the first one.

The second says, "E-e-h."

"Ah!" says the first one.

The second goes, "Mmm."

"Oh," nods the first.

"Ah-ha," says the second. *"S'iz azoy git zakh arooptseraidn fin hartsn.* It's so good to get it off my chest."

This isn't, however, a book of Yiddish theory; it's a book of Yiddish practice, a book about using the language yourself and understanding what's being said around you. It's designed to help you transform your experience of the world by making Yiddish a part of your daily life. Where my last book, *Born to Kvetch,* sought to describe the language and explain how it works, this one shows you what to do with it. If *Born to Kvetch* is Yiddish anatomy, *Just Say Nu* is a bodybuilding guide: it shows you how to flex the Yiddish muscles that *Born to Kvetch* describes.

"And why," you might ask, "do I need to pepper my conversation with words, phrases, entire sentences and paragraphs in a language that almost nobody really knows anymore?"

Why not? Yiddish has the unique ability to diminish human misery without providing any concomitant increase in happiness—and if you think that's easy, here's your chance to try it.

Don't look for standard western logic here; like any real conversation, the book is structured on the Talmudic principle of "that reminds me," which is why curses and descriptions of anger will be found in the section on driving—they've been included where they're most likely to come to mind and prove useful.

Transliteration

Yiddish is written in the Hebrew alphabet. There are a number of transliteration systems around, the most widely used being the one developed by YIVO, the Yidisher Visnshaftlikher Institut, the world's leading Yiddish academic institution. The YIVO system has a lot going for it and has been adopted as the standard by most universities and libraries. It can be confusing for nonspecialists, though; I've tried to go for something as close to English as possible, strange as things might sometimes end up looking. The only major exception to this refusal to follow the usual rules is found in the word *nu* itself; *noo*, which would have been consistent with the system that I've developed, looked so strange, so silly, so utterly un-Yiddish, that I couldn't bring myself to use it.

In actual passages of dialogue, I've used large capital letters to indicate the stressed syllables, and small capital letters to show the unstressed. "Bar mitzvah," for instance, would look like this: BAR-MITSveh. "Bas mitzvah," the female version, would be: BAS-MITSveh. Within the text, I've also used large and small capital letters with words that are being used for the *first time*, after which they're simply italicized. So, for example, "NEBAKH is a very important word. *Nebakh* can be said to be . . ."

Readers interested in trying to put their own dialogues together are advised to have a look at the appendix on Yiddish grammar that follows chapter 9.

A bigger problem is the matter of dialect. Most textbooks and official publications follow the standard language developed by YIVO and spoken by virtually no one. As the point of this book is to be able to understand the overwhelming majority of contemporary

Yiddish-speakers and to try to sound as much like a real Yiddish-speaker as possible, I've chosen to leave the YIVO system behind and simply transliterate things into the Polish Yiddish that I grew up speaking and continue to use today.

I've made a couple of slight modifications. Polish Yiddish was no more monolithic than American English; some pronunciations varied by region, some by social class. This is particularly true of the vowel that we find in the English *stay*; in some parts of Yiddish-speaking Poland, such a word would have rhymed with *day*; in others with *die*. In such cases, where there are equally valid choices within the dialect, I've used *ay* to represent the diphthong. It means that you can pronounce something like *stay* either as you just did or else as *sty*. Either is correct—just pick one and try to be consistent. Choose the one that's most comfortable for you—or decide how deeply old country (*stay*) or contemporary Brooklyn (that'd be the *sty* side) you wish to sound and then stay (or sty) with it.

The diphthong given here as *ei* has been borrowed from the YIVO version of the language; the way it's pronounced in my own dialect (a sort of long drawn-out *aaa* that is impossible to transcribe accurately without getting very technical) would have been too difficult to get across on the printed page.

Uncommon words are sometimes (and silently) given in their standard language versions, to help make sure that you're understood.

Vowels

a   as in *far*

e   the Yiddish short *e* is always like the vowel in *men* or *pet*; it never sounds like the *e* in *herd*—so the Yiddish *her* rhymes with *mare*, *bear*, not with English *her* or *sir*

ee   as in *feet* or the second vowel sound in *machine*

i   as in *hit*

o   as in *corn* or *or*

oo   as in *boot*

u   as in *hood, book, foot* (except in *nu*)

Diphthongs

ai   as in *plain*

ei   as in *mine*

ay pronounce as either *ai* or *ei*; choose one and go with it

Consonants

ch as in *chore*

kh as the first sound in *Chanukah*; it's the hard *h* at the end of J. S.
Bach

ts   as at the end of *chintz*

tsh as in *itch*

A Note on Translation, References, and Further Reading

Unless otherwise indicated, all translations are my own.

The two books to which this one makes frequent reference are both dictionaries and are both in print:

Alexander Harkavy, *Yiddish-English-Hebrew Dictionary* (Yale University Press, originally published, 1928).

Uriel Weinreich, *Modern English-Yiddish Yiddish-English Dictionary* (Schocken Books, originally published, 1968).

A couple of good introductory textbooks (if you're an intermediate or advanced student, you know enough to find your own textbooks) are:

Uriel Weinreich, *College Yiddish* (YIVO Institute for Jewish Research, sixth revised edition, 1999).

Sheva Zucker, *Yiddish: An Introduction to the Language* (Workmen's Circle Education Dept., 1995).

Readers looking for something less academically oriented should enjoy *The Complete Idiot's Guide to Learning Yiddish* by Rabbi Bernard Blech (Alpha Books, 2000).

Anybody interested in Yiddish should keep an eye out for Maurice Samuel's *In Praise of Yiddish* (Henry Regnery, 1971). It seems to be out of print at the moment, but copies are worth looking for in used-book stores and online.

I

Greeting and Meeting

Hello

It's supposed to be simple. An English greeting helps to move two people across the great divide from quiet to conversation, from separation to communication. You say *hello, good morning,* or *good evening,* and you get *hello, good morning,* or *good evening* in return. Each formula is a well-paved pathway, a gentle ramp that leads easily from one state of being to another.

A Yiddish greeting does nothing of the kind. Take a look at the most basic way of saying hello,

SHOOlem aLAYkhem,

which has a literal meaning of "peace upon you." Now compare it with the sole permissible response,

aLAYkhem SHOOlem,

and you'll see what you need to know from the start: *Yiddish conversation begins with a willingness to say the reverse of whatever has just been said to you*—even when you happen to agree. You're not *obliged* to disagree, but you have to be ready to do so: Yiddish conversations progress as much by means of rhetorical questions and outright contradiction as by supposedly direct logical paths leading from conversational point A to conversational point B. *Alaykhem shoolem* implies no disagreement, of course; Hebrew and Arabic both use almost identical greetings, but they don't use them as warm-ups for the gainsaying yet to come.

Don't be put off by this propensity to disagree; it's a good thing, and helps to mark the boundary between real conversation and random acts of speech. Simple speech acts—*raid*, they're called, "talk"—are as cheap in Yiddish as in any other language and tend not to be valued highly in a linguistic culture that prefers silence to lack of focus. *Raid* can be PISTEH, empty; HARBEH, strong or harsh; they can even be GESHLIFENEH, polished, and thus all the more slippery. The one thing they don't have to be is listened to:

MEH RAIT IN DER VELT AREIN

One speaks into the world,

means that you're talking to the void; your words are in vain because they are aimless, directed to no one. *Raid*—which Yiddish uses no less than any other language—are like kids at the recess bell or gays in the closet: they're going to come out, whether you want them to or not.

A *SHMOOS*,* on the other hand (the Yiddish rhymes with *loose*), a real conversation, begins with the idea of partnership. It's no accident that *shmoos* (pronounced *shmees* in the dialect used in this book—we don't even agree with ourselves, let alone anyone else) comes from a Hebrew word that means "tiding, rumor"; something that you've heard rather than something that you've said. Shmoozing is based on listening, on the idea of responding to what you hear and being answered in turn by someone who has been listening to you.

Disagreement leads to even closer attention. Heart speaketh to heart is very nice until all that treacle starts to cloy; heart yelleth at heart can be just as human and a lot more fun. Yiddish not only helped to inspire much of Martin Buber's work, it anticipated his idea of *Ich und Du*, "I and Thou," by hundreds of years. To be

---

* which usually appears in English as *schmooze* or *shmooze*.

sure, people who speak to each other in Yiddish spend much of their time in a sort of conversational collision, banging up against each other without ever going anywhere—just like people who are having sex. Contrary impulses and ideas pressing against each other can lead to communion and release—you don't *have* a shmooze in Yiddish, you *farFEER* one. The verb means "to seduce, to lead astray." *Meh farFEERT a shmees;* the meaningful exchange of words is a matter of enticement and persuasion.

The choice of verb here—the idiom means "to start or strike up an informal conversation"—gives us some insight into basic Yiddish notions of talk. While *farfeern* is frequently used to explain how girls get into trouble or yeshiva boys fall victim to the blandishments of the outside world, all that is seduced in a Yiddish conversation, all that is *farfeert* or derailed, is the selfish and ultimately silly desire for one absolute or the other: either total silence or total refusal to shut the hell up. Just as two willing bodies come together only because both have already said yes, so a real shmooze depends on consent, on each party agreeing to listen to what the other has to say. The average Yiddish shmooze involves two people who have renounced their claims to silence on the one hand and to monologue on the other. Each is willing to give the other a chance to do something other than daydream or obey— even though each already knows that the other must be wrong.

As such, not every exchange of dialogue attains the status of shmooze. Plenty of nudniks speak Yiddish, and fear of their all-consuming tedium often causes Yiddish to be spoken at a clip that makes even the most agitated English sound like a pothead's drawl; it's a sign that either party to a dialogue is afraid that *now* is their last chance to get a word in. The shmooze is there to keep us from treating everybody like a nudnik, and it is ironic that the current English use of *shmooze* has stood the Yiddish meaning on its head:

To chat in a friendly and persuasive manner especially so as to gain favor, business, or connections . . . <she *schmoozed* her professors>

This sort of careerist nudnik-ery, defined for us here by the eleventh edition of *Merriam-Webster's Collegiate Dictionary*, seems to be a recent development. Leo Rosten makes no mention of it in his entry for *schmooze* in *The Joys of Yiddish*, published in 1968, and I can't recall having heard it myself until some time in the 1990s. The overtone of purposeful friendliness, affability with an ulterior motive, couldn't be further from the feel of the original; it might be preferable to its purely English equivalent—*network* used as a verb, God forbid—but that doesn't bring it any closer to the Yiddish. Where real Yiddish obscenities like *shmok* and *potz* ("schmuck" and "putz") have turned cute in English, shmooze has been degraded from secular communion to self-serving sleaze. The transformation is ironic enough; it's even more ironic that English had to reinterpret a word from Yiddish—the language of eternal dissatisfaction—to characterize an essential stage toward getting what you want.

English speakers seek to satisfy their desires; all a Yiddish-speaker wants is a chance to open his mouth. A real shmooze involves an acknowledgment of the presence and importance of the person to whom you're speaking, which is why Yiddish leans so heavily on banter and wordplay; these apparently gratuitous remarks are there as conversational *Chanuka gelt*, tokens of esteem, little spoken gifts.

The importance of the other person also explains why there are no Yiddish versions of "your call is important to us" in this book. Even a strict textbook version would have to come with a question mark at the end: "Your call is important to us?" Yeah, sure. The shmooze version, the honest, no-bullshit rendition that should have been yours by right, is *Ven meh volt gevolt mit deer raidn, volt men mit deer shoyn gerait* (If we wanted to talk to you, we would be).

As with virtually all Yiddish greetings, *alaykhem shoolem* is often, though not inevitably, followed by a challenge in the form of *nu*, which has a basic meaning of "so" or "well," as if to say, "Now that we've got the hellos out of the way, what have you got to say for yourself? *Nu*—give some account of your activities, justify your presence on this planet." It is the prelude to "How are you?" or "What's doing?" (For more on *nu*, see page 28.)

While *nu* can be used as part of virtually any greeting, the response to other salutations is just as fixed as *alaykhem shoolem*. Greetings are classified by time of day, time of week, and time of the Jewish year, and God help anyone who doesn't use the precise formula called for on a Saturday evening when Sunday is one of the two closing days of Passover—they'll never be taken seriously again.

The basic weekday greetings are

GIT MORGN	GOT-ELF	GITN UVNT
good morning	*good afternoon*	*good evening.*

The Sabbath and other Jewish holidays have greetings of their own, which tend to be used even by people who would never think of observing them. These greetings are based on a rigid pecking order of holidays, in which Saturday trumps everything except for Yom Kippur:

Friday afternoon through Saturday:

GIT SHAbes
Good Sabbath

A holiday that falls on a Saturday:

GIT SHAbes, GIT YONtef
Good Sabbath, happy holiday

Saturday night:

GIteh VOKH
Good week

Saturday during the High Holiday season:

GIT SHAbes, GIT YONtef, GIT YOOR
Good Sabbath, happy holiday, happy new year

New moon:

GITN KHOYdesh
A good month

Holidays (except Purim and Chanukah):

GIT YONtef
Happy holiday

The intermediate days of Passover and Tabernacles:

GITN MOYed
Happy in-between times

It's as if "Merry Christmas" were a test, not a slogan. Newcomers to Yiddish can conceal their ignorance for a few extra seconds by taking advantage of the fact that every greeting, no matter how specialized, gets exactly the same response:

GIT YOOR
A good year.

Hence the well-known proverb: *Az meh git a yeedn a git morgn, git er oop a gants yoor,* "If you give a Jew a good morning, he gives you a whole year in return." Since no opening line conveys good wishes for more than a year, you can never go wrong by offering a year in return—a habit that also saves you from having to pay much attention to the person who's started talking.

Someone entering a home, a business, or an unusually hospitable kosher hotel with a Yiddish-speaking desk clerk will often be greeted with

BUrekh-a-BU

Blessed be the one who comes.

The sole proper response—one that separates the *yold* from the adept in the secrets of Yiddish—is

BUrekh-a-NIMtseh

Blessed be the one who is already here.

As a noun, burkh-A-beh (note the shift in stress and loss of an *e*) means "welcome, reception." A SHAYnem burkh-A-beh, "a lovely reception," means that you've been ignored, insulted, or attacked. If you should use the phrase while being physically ejected from someplace, it means "I had a yarmulke when I came in."

When the lights go up in the burlesque house and you find Rabbi Goldberg sitting next to you, all there is to say (assuming that you're the one who recovers quickly enough to speak first) is,

NU, RABBI, VOOS ZUGT EER GITS?

What's the good word, Rabbi? [lit., "What good do you say?"].

It means, "Nice to see you, but why am I seeing you here?" and indicates that you've run into someone in a place where they aren't expected to be. In less embarrassing circumstances—you own the burlesque house and know that Rabbi Goldberg knows that you do—it's a friendly way of asking someone what business has brought them to so unusual a location.

Good-bye

Thousands of pop songs to the contrary, it's always easier to say good-bye, which makes one wonder why Jews take so long to do so. There are only three greeting-and-response pairs in standard use, and the response—as you might already have expected—is the same in every case:

A GITN TUG	A GIтeн NAKHT	A GIтeн VOKH
good day	*good night*	*good week* (on Saturday night).

The all-purpose answer is

A GIT YOOR

a good year.

If you're trying to end a conversation or walk out of a room, the most common way to say good-bye is *ZEI* ᴳᵉ*ZINT* (literally, "be well"). If you're trying to get rid of a nudnik or have no plans of ever seeing someone again—so long as you can help it—you say *ZEI MEER* ᴳᵉ*ZINT* or even *ZEI-*ᶻʰᵉ *MEER* ᴳᵉ*ZINT*. The *meer* (which means "me") gives the expression a sense of "I hope that you're going to be healthy, because I have no intention of asking after you."

"*ZEI MEER* ᴳᵉ*ZINT MIT* [any noun you choose]" really means either, "Stop bothering me about whatever-it-is [because you're leaving]," or "You and your whatever-it-is-that-you-won't-stop-going-on-about can go to hell together." To someone who's about to embark on a trip, whether to the source of the Nile or the store on the corner, you say:

GAY geZINterHAYT	FOOR geZINterHAYT	FOOR geZINT IN KIM geZINT
Go in good health	*Travel in good health*	*Go and come back in good health.*

If they indicate that they're planning to go to a place that you've already warned them off of, *GAY (*or *FOOR) geZINterHAYT* can also mean, "Go ahead and go, but don't say that I didn't warn you"; "Go—whatever happens is your own damned fault."

How Are You?

Despite the fact that a polite evasion is as close as anyone is likely to come to a positive response to the question—if you don't get a kvetch, you'll get a circumlocution—Yiddish speakers continue to ask after one another's welfare as if they were gathering material for a long-term anthropological study of what can go wrong. Such behavior might be based on religious principles: the Mishna enjoins us to "Be the first to greet [that is, inquire after the welfare of] every man" (Ovos 4:16), but says nothing about hanging around to listen to his answer.

VOOS MAKHT EER?

How are you? (To a stranger, elder or social superior)

VOOS MAKHstee?

How are you? (To a friend, a child, anyone whom you outrank)

VOOS MAKHT A YEED?

How are you? [lit., "How is a Jew?" Used only between males; informal and synagogue usage]

VOOS MAKHT EER GITS?

How you doing, man/dude/pal o' mine?

The verb *makhn*, "to make," can also mean "to do, to say; to swing, to wave, to be":

VOOS MAKHT DEIN SHVESter?

How's your sister?

The textbook response would be

ZEE MAKHT GIT

She's (doing) well.

What you're far more likely to hear, assuming that she's really getting on all right, is

KEneh HOreh

or

keNAIneh HOreh,

variant pronunciations of a phrase that means "[may] no evil eye [befall her]" (see page 40), or the truly all-purpose

BU-rekh-a-SHEM

Thank God [lit., " blessed be God"],

the politest possible way of saying absolutely nothing.

The textbook response to any question about yourself,

GANTS GIT

very well,

is pretty much confined to textbook use and doesn't really do much to further conversation.

"I'm doing quite well, thanks. My children—they should live and be well—head up the only orthodox Junior Achievement Club in the state; my husband, the cardiologist/rabbi, has just been named America's first Jewish astronaut and will soon be taking *shabes* into outer space, *kenaineh horeh*; I've won the Nobel Prize for Economics *and* Home Economics, and Color Me Kosher, my it's-fun-to-be-*frum* cosmetics business, is the first glatt kosher firm to be named to the Fortune 500.

It's people like this for whom the evil eye was invented.

The more usual responses to general questions about your welfare are

NISHKOOSHEH	E-E-H
Not bad	*A less confident "not bad"*
FRAIG NISHT	AF MEINEH SONIM GEZUGT
Don't ask	*It should happen to my enemies.*

E-e-h and *nishkoosheh* are two of many Yiddish words with a pronounced physical component. In order to use either of them effectively:

1. Raise the right hand to mid-chest level, palm parallel to the floor.
2. Give the wrist a quarter-turn to the left (toward you), followed immediately by a half-turn right (i.e., a quarter-turn from the starting position), followed immediately by a half-turn left.
3. Repeat if needed with an extended *e-e-h* or every time that *nishkoosheh* is said.

A truly fantastic "greeting" that asks "How are you," provides a negative response on behalf of the person asked, and leaves them more room than ever to bend your ear with complaints is

Epes geFELstee MEER NISHT

I somehow don't like you, [i.e., *there's something about you that displeases me;* i.e., *I can see that there's something wrong with you, so why don't you tell me about it*].

The word *heint,* "today," is often appended to the phrase ("*Epes gefelstee meer nisht heint*") just to make sure that the person to whom it's addressed doesn't get the wrong idea. As mentioned above, this phrase is an invitation to kvetch and should never be used unless you really, really care.

Meeting

VEE HAYST EER?

What's your name? (formal)

VEE HAYstee?

What's your name? (informal)

MAH SHMAIkhem?

What's your name? (from the Hebrew. Faux formal; characteristic synagogue usage)

IKH HAYS . . .

My name is . . .

MEH RIFT MIKH . . .

Everyone calls me . . .

HAYSN HAYS IKH MAURICE, NOR RIFN RIFT MEN MIKH "THE SPACE COWBOY"

My name is really Maurice, but people call me the Space Cowboy.

baKEN ZAKH MIT MEIN MAN/FROY

Meet my husband/wife

LOmikh EIKH FOORshteln MEIN BREEder GEORGE

Let me introduce you to my brother George

ZAYer OONgeNAIM

Nice to meet you [lit., "very pleasant"]

ZAYer EINgeNImen
Nice to meet you [lit., "very welcome"]

DRIKN DEE HANT, "the shaking of hands" (literally, "pressing the hand") usually follows.

Simple Conversation: The Weather

MENDEL: S'IZ SHAYN IN DROYSN?
Is it nice out?

MINDEL: VEN SEH RAIGNT NISHT
If it doesn't rain.

MENDEL: S'IZ HAYS, HUH?
Hot, isn't it?

MINDEL: NISHT aZOY HAYS VEE FAYKHT
It ain't the heat, it's the humidity.

MENDEL: aZOY ZUGT MEER DER reMAtehs
My rheumatism tells me that.

MINDEL: MEER OYKH. IN HEYkher
Mine, too. And louder.

In order to discuss the weather effectively, it helps to be able to identify the following:

DAY AND NIGHT

TUG	NAKHT	LIKHtik	FINster
day	*night*	*light, bright*	*dark*

MEER IZ FINster geVORN IN DEE OYGN.
It went me dark in the eyes [i.e., *I was greatly dismayed.*]

HEAVENLY BODIES

HIML	ZEEN	leVOOneh
sky	*sun*	*moon*

SHAYN VEE DEE leVOOneh
Beautiful as the moon [i.e, *pretty as a picture*]

SHTERN	VOLKN	VOLKN-KRAtser
star	*cloud*	*skyscraper* [lit., "cloud scratcher"]

ZEI MOYKHL, IKH KISH DAIM HIML ITST
Excuse me while I kiss the sky [lit., "I'm kissing the sky now"].

BASIC PRECIPITATION

RAIGN	ES RAIGNT	SE PLYUkhet IN DROYSN
rain	*It's raining*	*It's pouring out there*

DIner	BLITS	BLITS-POST
thunder	*lightning*	*e-mail* [lit., "lightning post"]

SHNAY	ES SHNAYT
snow	*It's snowing*

AN aVAYreh A HINT aROYStseTREIBM
Not fit for a dog outside [lit., "It'd be a sin to put a dog out"]

EIZ	GLITSHN ZAKH
ice	*to slip, slide, skate*

A distinction that shouldn't be overlooked:

MEER IZ HAYS	MEER IZ KALT
I'm hot	*I'm cold*

but

IKH BIN HAYS	IKH BIN KALT
I'm horny	*I'm frigid*

There's nothing more embarrassing than sitting in a stuffy room and saying, "Am I the only one here who's horny?" without even knowing that you've done so.

Common Courtesy

Those who think of Yiddish-speakers as rude will be shocked to discover that Yiddish has two ways of saying *please* that people who speak the language use all the time:

ZEI/ZEIT ʌZOY GIT	and	IKH BAIT DIKH/EIKH
[lit., "Be so good"]		[lit., "I beg you, I pray you"].

Many of the same people are, however, just as likely to point at something that they want and grunt, generally from somewhere behind the nose (grunting of this sort seems to be a male prerogative), or else shout out the name of whatever it is that's wanted, for instance, *"ZALTS!"* (Salt!) or *"GATkehs!"* (Long johns!) with a strong if unspoken sense of "now."

No one reading this book will be able to get away with such behavior until the generation just described has been gone long enough to be remembered by no one else. Until then, it's best to observe the proprieties and ask nicely:

	ZEIT ʌZOY GIT IN derLANGT
ZEIT ʌZOY GIT IN . . .	MEER DEE MIlekh
Please . . . [perform some action]	*Please pass me the milk*

HER SHOYN OYF,	HALTS MOYL,	TEE MEER NISH'
IKH BAIT DIKH	le-MAN-ʌ-SHEM	KA' TOYvehs
Please stop already	*Shut up, for God's sake*	*Don't do me any favors.*

It's also considered good form to say *thank you*:

A DANK EIKH	YAsher KOYekh	A GROYSN DANK
Thanks/thank you	*Thanks* [lit., "may	*Thanks very much;*
	your strength increase"]	*thanks a lot.*

And let's not forget *you're welcome:*

adeRAbeh	nishTOO FAR VOOS	ZOL ES DEER VOYL baKIMen
You're welcome [lit., "on the contrary"]	*You're welcome* [lit., "there's nothing to thank me for"]	*Enjoy it; use it in good health* [lit., "may it be very agreeable to you"].

FOR-FRIGGIN-GIVENESS

ZEIT MOYKHL, which has a very literal meaning of "forgive me," really means "excuse me, I beg your pardon" or "please." If you want to ask a stranger for directions, you approach with ZEIT MOYKHL, "excuse me"; you say the same thing if you're pushing your way through a row of seated theater-goers with a box of popcorn in your hand. If you want someone to pass you the milk and you don't feel like using ZEI(T) AZOY GIT, you could say ZEIT MOYKHL, DEE MILEKH, "milk, please." It gets more interesting, though, when you find yourself in the usual Yiddish situation of not getting what you want: you've tried a couple of *zeit azoy gits* and the damned *milekh* is still at the other end of the table. You can then say IKH BIN DEER MOYKHL DEE MILEKH—literally, "I forgive you in regards to the milk." What it really means is "You can take your stinking milk and pour it through a funnel where the sun don't shine." Or you can reach over, invade the personal space of the *yutz* who's ignoring your request, take the milk yourself and say MOYKHL, "Don't friggin' bother."

You can use MOYKHL even more ironically to indicate how little you want something that's been offered you: VILST ESN BAY MEER KREPlakh, "Want a knuckle sandwich?" (Literally, "Would you like me to give you some dumplings to eat?") Just hold up your hands and say, MOYKHL, "[No] *thanks!*"

MEKHEELEH, the noun derived from *moykhl,* means "pardon" or "forgiveness," what you ask for on Yom Kippur. It's also used to mean *TUKHES* or "rear end":

VILST A KOPEH IN MEKHEELEH AREIN?
Want a kick right up your you'll-pardon-the-expression?

MOYKHL
No *thanks!*

Forms of Address

Like most people with no real power, Yiddish-speakers are obsessed with respect and are quick to take umbrage when they feel improperly treated. Many misunderstandings arise simply from calling someone DEE—the familiar (and singular) form of the second person pronoun—rather than EER, its polite (and plural) version.

People with whom you use DEE:

Family members

Friends

Classmates, former classmates

Contemporaries whom you meet in social settings

Colleagues who don't outrank you

Anyone whom you outrank (unless DEE could provoke embarrassing rumors: use EER with your personal assistant)

All children

Pets

Anyone whom you're busy insulting

God

Eer is for everyone else, until such time as you both agree to *dee*. The old man behind the counter whom you've addressed as *dee* is going to feel much like an African-American man who's just been called *boy*—don't expect him to do you any favors.

Starting a conversation with *eer*, though, can be like beginning with "Hey, mister!" in English. You can address men as REB YEED, "sir," (literally, "Mr. Jew") or even DER YEED, "the Jew," i.e., "the gentleman." With women, all you've got to work with is MRS. (which is Yiddish for "Ma'am" in English-speaking countries), while kids can be addressed as YINGL, MAYDL, or BUkheR, depending on whether the kid is a boy, a girl or a boy over thirteen. The kids, of course, are addressed as *dee*. Older people can be addressed quite properly as FEter OR MEEmeh, uncle or aunt, whether they're related to you or not. *Zeit moykhl, feter*, "Excuse me, uncle," or *A dank eikh, meemeh*, "Thank you, auntie," are perfectly polite when dealing with people eligible for pensions, and are highly recommended for daily use: the fastest way to provoke a fight in Yiddish is to fail to defer to someone who is older than you. As we'll see very shortly, we're dealing with a culture that thinks of aging as an act of virtue.

A Few Common Yiddish Words
That Don't Fit in Anywhere Else

YO	NAYN	AZOY	EFsheR
yes	*no*	*yes; so; thus*	*maybe*
VER	**VOOS**	**VEE**	**VEN**
who	*what*	*where*	*when*
FAR VOOS	**VEE AZOY**	**TAIkef**	**BALD**
why	*how*	*right away*	*soon, right away*

Five Little Words That Will Get You Through Any Yiddish Conversation

1. NU

The following conversation *could* take place in what anybody who wants to speak Yiddish without actually learning it might consider the best of all possible Yiddish-speaking worlds, the one where no sentence is longer than a single word. Imagine two speakers, A and B, discussing the health of a gravely ill acquaintance:

> A: NU?
> *Well—?*

> B: SHOYN.
> *It's all over.*

> A: Epes—?
> *Something [in the way of a turn for the worse befell him that he wasn't healthy enough to be able to withstand]?*

> B: TAkeh.
> *Precisely.*

> A: NEbakh.
> *That's too bad.*

Add the proper tones to these five little words, and the dialogue is no longer quite as scanty as it looks on the page. How can a language with so many speakers who never stop talking leave so much space for taciturnity? Because those speakers know that you *know;* and they know that you know that *they* know.

Many years ago I strayed into a strange synagogue, looking for a minyen to say kaddish. I'd no sooner passed through the door than the SHAmes, the synagogue-version of a top sergeant, cornered me and asked point-blank, *"Vee, fin, voos?"* (How, from, why?) That is, *Vee haystee, fin vanet kimstee, voos tistee doo:* "What's your name, where are you from, and what are you doing here?"

The *shames* wasn't being rude; he was working. So brutally circumcised a conversation could only take place in a synagogue, where rigid if generally unrecognized conventions govern the initial course of conversation with strangers. Since context had already determined what had to follow each of the words that the *shames* uttered, it was easy to know what he meant and to respond accordingly.

The five little words that we'll be looking at over the course of this book are the opposite of the *shames*'s *vee, fin,* and *voos.* Each has so wide a range of possible meanings that it can do duty for entire sentences. You will sound totally au courant, thoroughly Yiddish-savvy, even though you might not have any idea of what you're talking about, what's going on around you, or why people are responding to you in the way that they are. These words are a safe and effective substitute for alcohol and drugs, and you can use them as often as you like. ❧

Among the best-known words in the language, *nu* is sometimes heard in English these days, but rarely among non-Jews and never with the vast range of meaning that it can have in Yiddish. Things have changed considerably since 1958 or '59 when I went tearing out of the room where I'd been watching *December Bride* in order to inform my mother that Pete Porter, one of the regular characters, had to be Jewish. Pete was played by Harry Morgan (who was also Bill Gannon on *Dragnet* and Colonel Potter on *M*A*S*H*), and anyone who's seen the show will remember that its characters were among the most irredeemably *goyish* in an era of irredeemably *goyisheh* sitcoms. My mother, ever the diplomat, asked me how I knew. *"Er hot nor voos gezugt nu,"* I told her. "He just said *nu.*" My mother didn't miss a beat. *"Iz nu?"* she asked, as if to say, "And what? He shouldn't say *nu?*"

Nu is that kind of word. According to Uriel Weinreich, *nu* means "Go on! well? come on!" And it does. But it can mean so very much more, depending on context and tone of voice.

At its most colorless, *nu* can be used to link two disparate elements in a conversation, as when you want to change from one subject to another and can't think of a smooth transition, or want to resume speaking after a long silence, comfortable or not. In a sentence like,

> . . . IN IZ PLIᴛꜱɪᴍ ɢᴇSHTORBM.
>
> NU, LOᴍᴇᴇʀ RAIDN FIN FRAYʟᴇᴋʜᴇʀᴇʜ ZAKHN
>
> *. . . and died suddenly. **Nu**, let's speak of happier matters,*

the happy matter could be a Mets victory or a warmer day than you'd expect for November; the point is that the *nu* gets you out of any topic that's become unpleasant, uncomfortable, or uninteresting and serves as a magic bridge to whatever you'd like to discuss next. You could just as easily say,

> . . . IN IZ PLIᴛꜱɪᴍ ɢᴇSHTORBM.
>
> NU, IKH HOB NEKHTN OOPɢᴇFRAIGT EINSTEIN'S ᴛᴀɪORʏᴇʜ
>
> *. . . and died suddenly. **Nu**, I disproved Einstein's theory yesterday,*

as go on to a eulogy of the deceased. A *nu* of this type must follow seamlessly from the preceding word, as if it's merely the final syllable: ɢᴇ-*SHTORBM-NU*. (The bold type above is intended as an aid to *nu*-location; it has nothing to do with accent or stress.)

This sort of *nu* is closely related to the "Let's stick to the matter at hand" *nu*, as seen in such phrases as

NU, VOOS VET ZEIN?	or	NU, ʀᴀBOYꜱᴇɪ
Nu, what's going to be?		*Nu, gentlemen.*

These are used in order to get things back on track (at a meeting, for instance) after some digression in the proceedings. They mean, "That's all well and good, but what about the main point"; or, "Leaving aside everything that's been raised hitherto, let's return to the central question of . . ."

Nu, raboysei can also be used as a way of calling a group of people to order or getting a meeting or assembly under way. It's a more refined way of clearing your throat or saying, "Let's cut the crap and get down to business."

Nu can also be used on its own as a way of opening and even sustaining a conversation. You can approach a Yiddish-speaking stranger almost anywhere and simply say,

NU-U-U?

Translated briefly, this would mean, "What are you doing here and what have you got to say for yourself?" Such an introduction could theoretically lead to the following exchange:

THEM: NU!?
What business is it of yours and who are you that you should even be asking?

YOU: NU!!
I demand an answer!

THEM: IZ NU?
Is that a fact?

At which point the other person turns on her heel and leaves. Although such a conversation is possible (and when dealing with "life of the party" types, all too probable), there's a general feeling that two unaccompanied *nu*s in succession are more than enough for any conversation.

The *iz nu* with which the above exchange ends is, of course, exactly what my mother said on hearing that Pete Porter was Jewish. Context determines the precise meaning of the phrase. When my mother used it, she meant, "What else should he have said?

Tell me something surprising." Immediately above, it means, "I know that you want an answer and I don't care one little bit." In short, "So what?" It can be a friendly "so what," as in "That's exactly what I would have expected," or a hostile "so what," as in, "tough noogies":

> YOU: DER NAZI HOT ɢᴇRAIT VEE AN ANᴛᴇᴇ-ꜱᴇMIT.
> *The Nazi spoke like an anti-Semite.*

> THEM: IZ NU?
> *And? . . .*

or

> YOU: MEER ɢᴇFELT NISHT DEIN ARʙᴇᴛ.
> *I don't like your work.*

> THEM: IZ NU?
> *So what's it to me?*

This usage shades almost imperceptibly into the *nu* of utter indifference, the "is that supposed to be of any interest" *nu*:

> SAM SPADE: IKH HOB ɢᴇZAIN JOEL CAIRO HEINT BEI NAKHT.
> *I saw Joel Cairo tonight.*

> MISS O'SHAUGHNESSY: NU?
> *So?*

Nu can also be used to preface a question with which you'd like to begin a conversation:

> NU, VOOS MAKHT A YEED?
> *Nu, how's a Jew?*

is like saying, "So how's it going?" in English. The *nu*, like the *so*, helps to soften the question and indicate an openness to further conversation. It's as if you're saying, "Ah, there you are. I've been wondering about you lately."

The *nu* of impatience is among the most prominent of all the *nu*s, and is probably the most frequently heard. It starts with a simple

NU-U-U?

Come on,

delivered in a tone midway between quizzical and chagrined, as if to say, "If you don't know what the gas pedal is there for, how did you get so far in this traffic to start with?" It's a "poop or get off the pot" sort of thing. *Nu* here means "either do it or don't do it, but make a decision and let us know":

KIMST TSEE NISHT? NU?

Are you coming or not? Make up your mind, commit yourself
to one course of action or the other.

The next step up from the simple *nu* of impatience involves linking *nu* with another of the five most useful Yiddish words, *shoyn*:

NU, SHOYN?

Come on, already.

Imagine an old movie, one of those where the bad guy, secure about the good guy's goodness, hands him his gun and says, "Go ahead, then, shoot me. Right here, in cold blood. Here, go ahead and shoot." If the movie were in Yiddish, the next line, the one right before, "Can't do it, can you? I didn't think you could," would be

NU, SHOYN?

Whatever it is, just do it already.

It should therefore come as no surprise that

NU, GAY SHOYN

Come on, go already,

is a favorite of Yiddish-speaking drivers the world over, or that no Nike commercial will ever be translated into Yiddish. "Just do it" runs the marathons that its translation, *nu shoyn,* never would.

Nu shoyn differs slightly from the closely related *nu-zhe,* which is a little less forthcoming, a little more beseeching. In the scenario just described,

NU-ZHE

would have more the sense of "Please shoot and put me out my misery" than "I double-dog dare you." Otherwise, it's more along the lines of "*Nu,* please," than the overtly imperative *nu shoyn.*

Nu can also indicate that things have come to an end, even when those things are only your patience.

NU, LOmeer GAYN
Nu, let's go

can mean either, "Oh, have we finished? Then let's be on our way," or "Okay. That's it! I can't take any more. Let's go." You could also use it if you and a friend were suddenly to be given an invitation to a party; in such a case, *nu* would have a sense very like that of "okay."

Nu can even be used to mean "if." If a friend is afraid that her ex-husband might show up at some social event to which she's been invited, you can say,

NU, AZ ER KIMT IZ VOOS *[best pronounced here as* VOO-es
for the sake of contemptuous emphasis]?
And if he comes, so what?

Without the *nu,* the sentence wouldn't have so strong a sense of "so what, it doesn't matter."

If you ask a kid, or a roomful of kids, "Want candy?" expect to hear a response of

NU, YEH!
We sure do!

This is a highly developed form of the "what else?" motif that we saw earlier and leads to the truly wonderful

POter NU
absolutely, undoubtedly, no question about it.

It's a response—arguably the best possible response—to a ridiculously obvious question. "Mr. Wex, do you know any members of the Jewish faith?" *"Poter nu!"* While the basic meaning of *poter* is "exempt from, free," here it means "of course, absolutely, for sure." *Poter nu* is really *poter; nu?* "Of course, why would you even think to ask?"

I've also been told that in many a marriage, a late-night, slightly diffident

NU?

often accompanied by a shrug (and usually uttered by the husband), is still considered foreplay. In other bedrooms, of course, the *nu* of impatience is used.

2

Stages of Life

"INTER *faeces et urinam nascimur*," wrote Saint Augustine, who just became the first Church Father ever quoted in a guide to Yiddish conversation. "We are born between feces and urine," he says, so let's not get carried away with ourselves; the birth canal through which all of us enter this world is located between the anus and the urethra, and we emerge from the womb as mired in physical filth as we are in original sin.

Had Augustine been born a few centuries later, he could have had quite a future in the greeting card business. Had he remembered that we pee at birth and poo at death, he might have got feces and urine in the proper order; his failure to do so explains why he is a Father of the Church and not a President of the Shul.

Any Yiddish-speaker can tell you that most human beings start their lives as PIshers and end them as ALTEH KAkers. For a Yiddish-speaking Jew, life is one long trip to the toilet, in which extremes of youth and age are expressed in terms of evacuation. A *pisher*, or "pisser," is wet behind the ears and everywhere else. (When the ears—and everything else—are feminine, the *pisher* is called a PISH-ERKEH.) When not an actual child, the *pisher* is a babe in the woods, a mere beginner, someone who has yet to learn his way around. It's offensive to have to compete with him, intolerable to have to submit:

OT DER PIsher VERT MIR ITST A BAleBOOS?
That pisher is gonna be my boss now?

ER HOT NOKH MIlekh AF DI VONtses.
He still has milk in his mustache.

ER'T LERnen AN ALTN TATN KINder MAKHN?

He's gonna teach a longtime [lit., "old"] *father how to make children?*

KH'OB SHOYN AF DAIM MEIneh TSAYN OYFgeGESN

I have eaten my way through my teeth while doing it [i.e., "Whatever it is,
I've been doing it for so long that my activity in the area has long
outlasted all the teeth that I had when I started"].

As baby boomers prepare to collect their pensions, Yiddish's
longstanding rejection of the modern cult of youth stands an excellent chance of returning to the cultural mainstream, where it
can offer practical tips on finding fault with any action performed by anyone not old enough to have bought a mono copy of
Sgt. Pepper on the day of its release. Yiddish doesn't dislike youth
per se, just youth that's been young since the speaker was; a
Yiddish-speaker knows everything you do—and a few things
that you've never even heard of—because, as he or she will be
quick to tell you,

'KH BIN NISHT NEKHTN aROYS FIN DEE VINdelakh

I wasn't toilet-trained [lit., "didn't get out of diapers"] *yesterday,*

or

IKH BIN NISHT KA' meLOOPM-KINT

I'm no babe in the woods.

Use a phrase like *meloopm-kint* and

MEH VET DEER OOPgaibm KOOved

People will render you the respect to which you're entitled,

they'll give you your props when it comes to speaking Yiddish.

Meloopm is the Hebrew name for a vowel with the sound of an
oo. Since most contemporary Yiddish-speakers have no idea what
a *meloopm* has to do with youth or innocence, this can be your

chance to show them who's boss. *Meloopm* comes from the Aramaic *meloh poom*, "a full mouth," and the term *meloopm-kint* is generally explained by the fact that the *meloopm* is very small, as is any kid who's just learning to read it, an explanation that might make sense if the *meloopm* were the only, or even the first, vowel that kids are taught in school, or if the phrase were ever used to describe actual children.

ER IZ NISHT KEN meLOOPM-KINT

He's no meloopm-kint

means that nobody's going to put anything over on him, because he's seen the world and is perfectly able to look out for himself. What it does not mean is that he's seven years old, rather than three.

OY, A rakhMOOnes AF IM, DAIM BIDnem meLOOPM-KINT

I feel sorry for him, the poor, innocent meloopm-kint

indicates that the poor sap is walking into a lion's den where he's going to be eaten alive, rather like Jimmy Stewart in *Mr. Smith Goes to Washington*.

So why a *meloopm*? What does a Hebrew vowel have to do with it? Make the sound that it represents—"Oo, oo," as Gunther Toody used to say—and watch what happens to your lips (people like me, who actually say *meleepm*, can observe the same phenomenon, thanks to the *l*). The rounded lips and sucking motion produce an image of youth and inexperience; *meloopm* conveys the sense of "suckling" or "baby." *Meloh poom* means a full mouth, and a literal *meloopm-kint* has a mouth full of mommy.

Expressions like this allow you to show everyone around you that, whatever else you might be, you're no *pisher* when it comes to Yiddish. So why cut their suffering short? Toy with them a little, let them know that their comeuppance is at hand by saying,

IKH'L DEER VEIZN VER S'IZ ELter

I'll show you who's boss [lit., "who's older"].

Older is *always* better in Yiddish; *elter* is used so unambiguously to mean "important" that you can actually say such things as

A KINT IZ ELter FIN A KAYser

A child [i.e., *one of your own*] *is older than* [i.e., *takes precedence over*] *an emperor,*

without anybody blinking an eye.

A Few Empty Threats

Ikh'l deer veizn ver s'iz elter is only one of a great many nonspecific yet utterly empty threats that punctuate so much Yiddish discourse; they are the barroom brawls of a culture that gets verbal rather than physical. The power of these threats lies entirely in the fact that no one—including the threatener—has any clear idea of what's really being said. English is no stranger to idioms of this sort—think of classics like "I'll give you something to cry about"; "you'll wish you'd never been born"; and "I'll have your guts for garters"—but it tends not to use them in adult conversations outside of the workplace. Among the Yiddish staples we find

IKH'L DIKH LERnen derkh-ERets
I'll teach you respect

and

IKH'L LERnen MIT DEER BOOlek
I'll teach you the Torah portion about Balak and Balaam
[i.e., *a lesson you'll never forget*].

These two are particularly popular when dealing with children. *Lernen derkh-erets* should be self-explanatory; *Boolek* refers to the

Torah portion that runs from Numbers 22:2–25:9, in which Balak, the king of Moab, hires Balaam, a freelance mage and shaman, to curse the Israelites. Try as Balaam might, though, every curse comes out as a blessing; his donkey speaks and Balak stiffs him for his fee—and if you think that nothing worked out right for *him*, wait till you see what I do with you:

VET ZAKH TEEN KHOYshekh (DOO/DORTN)
All hell's going to break loose (here/there).

An all-time favorite—great for kids and uncooperative clerks alike. From the Hebrew for "darkness," *khoyshekh* appears to have acquired the additional sense of "chaos, upheaval" from the Midrash, which describes how the Israelites took advantage of the plague of darkness (which affected only the Egyptians) to bury the turncoats in their midst, whom God didn't want to kill while the Egyptians were looking.

Another classic, one with a really creepy sense of dementia to it, is

BIST BEI MEER A geTSAITLter /geTSAITLteh
You (masc./fem.) *are on my list.*

It's like a Yiddish prophecy of Richard Nixon, dating from long before Nixon was born.

Some winners among threats promising specific acts of violence are

IKH'L ZEE MAKHN MIT A KOP KERtser
I'll make her a head shorter,

IKH'L IM tseSHNEIDN AF SHTIker
I'll cut him to pieces,

IKH'L DIKH tseTRAYbern
I'll beat the crap out of you [lit., "remove the unkosher
fat and veins from your carcass"].

Old Age

The idea that age alone is enough to make you important is fundamental to traditional Jewish life, and people are always wanting to know how old you are, especially if you're unmarried.

> **VEE ALT ZENT EER?**
>
> *How old are you?*

is the standard "secular" way of asking a person's age. If you're dealing with much older people, you'll usually say

> **VEE ALT IZ DER YEED, BIZ HINdert IN TSVONtsik?**
>
> *How old is the Jew, may he live to be a hundred and twenty?*

The *yeed,* of course, works only with men. You can use *feter* and *meemeh,* "uncle" and "aunt" (see page 26,) to get around this problem by asking, *Vee alt zent eer, feter* or *Vee alt zent eer, meemeh?* before you go on to add the bit about 120 years. Should you forget the age limit (which God sets as the maximum human lifespan in Genesis 6:3) or underestimate the traditionalism of the person to whom you're talking, they'll be sure to put it in for you:

> **IKH BIN ALT DRAY-IN-ZIbetsik, BIZ HINdert IN TSVONtsik YOOR**
>
> *I'm seventy-three, may I live for a hundred and twenty years,*

to which you respond with our old friend

> **KEneh HOreh/keNAIneh HOreh**
>
> *No evil eye.*

Alt can cover age in all its many meanings, from simple accumulation of years to utter decrepitude. In that sense, it isn't much different from "old" in such English expressions as "six years old"—

> **ALTer MAN**   **ALTeh FROY**
>
> *old man*   *old woman.*

You can even use the adjective on its own:

MEIN ALter/ALteh

my old man/woman.

Mein alter/alteh is far warmer and more friendly than "my old man" or "my old lady" would be in English. It's often used of relatively young people, and is really a way of blessing your spouse with a wish for long life.

Things are a little different with the diminutive, though. Without *mein* in front, ALtitshker and ALtitshkeh are closer to "little old man" and "little old lady" than to "senior citizen," and are often used pejoratively to suggest feebleness, incapacity, or age-related shock:

NOKH HINderter HAYseh BLITSpostn,

After hundreds of hot e-mails,

HOBM MEER SOF-SOF OOPgeMAKHT ZAKH TSE TREFN

we finally arranged to meet

BEIM IKEA IN kefeTEERyeh.

in the Ikea cafeteria.

KIMT OYS AZ DER INterNETer CHARLES BOYER

It turns out that the Charles Boyer of the Internet

IZ GOOR AN ALtitshker IN VEIseh SHEEKH IN A haVAee HEMD.

is really a little old man in white shoes and a Hawaii shirt.

The Mishna classifies the degrees of old age slightly more systematically:

At sixty you're ready for old age; at seventy for fullness of years; the tough ones get to eighty; at ninety you're stooped over; a one-hundred-year-old is as dead, as if he had passed away and ceased from the world (Ovos 5:21).

The connection of eighty with toughness is based on a statement in Psalm 90, which says in verse 10:

> The years of our life are threescore and ten, or fourscore by reason of strength [*GVEEres*]; and their pride [i.e., all they have to boast about] is but toil and trouble; they soon pass and we fly away.

Note the built-in *kvetch*—what's the point of staying alive if all the years bring is more *TSOOres*? It's in biblical passages like this that we find the roots of the Yiddish outlook on life, and this verse has entered day-to-day Yiddish in the phrase *EEber DEE GVEEres*, "beyond the [boundary marked by] strength," to refer to people in their eighties:

ER IZ SHOYN LANG EEber DEE GVEEres

He's long past the gveeres

means that he won't be seeing eighty again. A person who has passed the *gveeres* is what is known as a *YOOshish,* a very old person, one who's reached a venerable old age, as in, "You're *how* old?"

Yooshish is a highly respectable term, however. For all that Yiddish might be said to privilege age over youth, it's still full of pejorative terms for the elderly that are often used by the elderly themselves:

BUbeh, VEE aZOY FEELstee ZAKH HEINT?

How are you feeling today, Granny?

Some likely answers:

ALT

Old

OY, IKH BIN AN ALter SHKRAB

I'm a worn-out old shoe.

Bubbies who *wish* that they felt well enough to call themselves worn-out shoes are likely to use a popular image borrowed from the High Holiday liturgy:

IKH BIN NISHT MER VEE A ᴛꜱᴇBRUKHᴇɴᴇʀ **SHARBM**
I'm nothing more than a piece of a broken old pot.

The best-known pejorative term for the aged, though, is used only about others. *KAᴋᴇʀ* (rhymes with "sucker") literally, someone who is making number two, is more commonly used to mean someone whose every activity turns to crap, the sort of person whom Yiddish also calls a *ʟᴏʏ-YOOTSʟᴇᴋʜ,* "success-challenged" (sometimes punningly translated as "*oy,* useless"), because he can't seem to bring anything to fruition. *Alter kaker* is often abbreviated to A.K. in English, as Ira Gershwin does in *Of Thee I Sing*:

They're the A.K.'s who give the O.K.'s
One, two, three, four,
Five, six, seven, eight, nine,
Supreme Court judges—

The A.K. is an old man who sort of futzes along, dithering and doddering and always out of step. The *kaker*

DRAYT ZAKH VEE A FOORTS IN ROOSL
blunders around like a fart in the brine; has no idea where he's going
or what he's doing there.

The phrase would be a staple of dramatic criticism, if such criticism were still being written in Yiddish. *Roosl* is broth, brine, or pickle (the liquid you use to turn a cucumber into a gherkin). *Roosl-flaysh* is Yiddish for "pot roast," but more to the point here, *lign in roosl* means "to be in a pickle."

LAUREL: ᴀVEE ɢᴇFINᴇɴ MEER ZAKH ITST, OLʟɪᴇ?
Where are we now, Ollie?

HARDY: MEER LIGN IN ROOSL, STANley, NUKH A MOOL IN ROOSL.
We're in a pickle, Stanley, we're in another pickle.

The fart doesn't know what it's doing in the brine, but its frantic activity is stirring up a lot of bubbles that the pickles don't need.

Once an *alter kaker* is *eeber dee gveeres,* he is in serious danger of becoming *OYver-BOOTL,* senile. The term comes from the Mishnaic description of a one-hundred-year-old as being like someone who is dead, "passed away and ceased"—think of the English "past it" with a very similar meaning:

IKH ZAI VOOS DEE TIST DORTN—

I see what you're doing over there—

'KH BIN NOKH NISHT OYver-BOOTL

I haven't lost it yet.

NUMBERS

They'll never know how old you are if you don't know how to count. The basic Yiddish numbers are:

1.	AYNS, AYN (*ayns* is used in counting; *ayn* is followed by a noun)
2.	TSVAY
3.	DREI
4.	FEER
5.	FInef
6.	ZEKS
7.	ZEEBM
8.	AKHT

9.	NEIN
10.	TSEN
11.	ELEF
12.	TSVELEF
13.	DREITSN
14.	FERTSN
15.	FIFTSN
16.	ZEKHTSN
17.	ZEEBETSN
18.	AKHTSN
19.	NEINTSN
20.	TSVONTSIK
21.	AYNS-IN-TSVONTSIK
22.	TSVAY-IN-TSVONTSIK
30.	DREISIK
40.	FERTSIK
50.	FIFTSIK
60.	ZEKHTSIK
70.	ZEEBETSIK
80.	AKHTSIK
90.	NEINTSIK
100.	HINDERT
1,000.	TOYZNT

Terms of Endearment

The three little spits that keep most Yiddish compliments and good wishes from turning into their opposites aren't appropriate in every circumstance, and speakers are often afraid of the consequences that can follow in the wake of an unguarded compliment. Yiddish *wants* to be nice, but doesn't always know how: given a choice between mundane courtesy and metaphysical safety, Yiddish chooses safety every time. If expressing love and approbation might cause sinister forces to harm the object of love or destroy what has just been approved, then love and approbation are best indicated obliquely—generally by *not* indicating dislike or dissatisfaction. Such an approach is so taken for granted that guarded praise or even simple description can be used to express wild enthusiasm and endless love:

A KINT? OY, bisTEE A KINT. A KINT, A KINT, A KINT—VAY geVALT,

A KINT FIN KINderLANT

A child? Oy, are you a child. A child, a child, a child—goodness
gracious, a child from Childrenland.

A mother who speaks to her baby in this way is saying nothing—or almost nothing, given the uncertain location of Childrenland—that isn't a matter of incontrovertible fact. In a religion whose deity calls Himself, "I am what I am," calling things by their names can be the most exalted form of speech.

The following list contains most of the more common endearments and pet names. Note how solid they are; note how none of them can be made to mean its opposite. Their solid physicality—the fact that they're all concrete nouns rather than adjectives or verbs—means that there's nothing any wicked spirit or evil eye can do but accept them as they are. The opposite of *good* is *bad*; the opposite of *love* is *hate*; but the heart has no opposite, only a counterpart:

nehSHOOmenyu	HARTSeleh
dear little soul	*little heart.*

These are all-purpose, very intense endearments. They can be used of a lover, spouse, or child (as long as it's your own). They're somehow "wrong," though, coming from a child to a parent.

Just as intense, but much more versatile, the term *laibm*—"life"—can be added to a proper name or a term that describes a family relationship. In such cases, it means "dear" or "darling." Although it's been weakened a bit by overuse, the idea that you owe your continued existence to the person to whom you're speaking (*laibm* is used only in the second person), has something very appealing about it:

MENDL-LAIBM	chrisTINE-LAIBM
Mendel dear	*Christine dear*
MAmeh-LAIBM	TAteh-LAIBM
Mother dear	*Father dear.*

As in English, a number of endearments come from the animal world:

KETSeleh	TEIbeleh	FAYgeleh
pussy cat	*little dove*	*little bird.*

Ketseleh is a standard romantic diminutive, equivalent to the English "baby," "darling," "sweetie-pie," "honey," and so on. *Teibeleh* is only slightly less common and a little less versatile. While no one is likely to complain that The Four Tops' "Sugar pie, honeybunch," would come out as something like *"Ketseleh, teibeleh"* in Yiddish, fans of contemporary Christian music might have some trouble with a language that turns a phrase like "darling Jesus" into "Jesus, my little pussy cat."

Faygeleh, once quite common when talking to small children, has all but vanished as an endearment in English-speaking countries, where—probably under the influence of "faggot"—it has come to be used as a pejorative term for a gay man.

Inanimate objects aren't overlooked, either:

GOLD	OYTSER	KROYN
gold	*treasure*	*crown.*

These are especially effective when attached to the name of the person to whom you're speaking: Jimmy-OYTSER, Tiffany-KROYN.

Two of the stranger-looking endearments are:

TAteleh	MAmeleh
little father	*little mother.*

While especially common when speaking to children, these can both be used of adults, too, as a sign of real affection (compare the English "baby") or equivalents for "dad," "pal," "mac," "toots," or "babe" in direct address. Both terms are examples of the disguised blessings that are so prominent in Yiddish: when you call a child "little father" or "little mother," you're wishing that it live long enough to become a parent itself. Although the show-biz *bubbie* that was once so common really comes from the German *Bube,* "boy" (which comes into English as *bub,* as in "What's all the hubbub, bub?"), the German original was assimilated to the Yiddish *BUbeh,* which means "grandmother," and then reinterpreted as yet another Yiddish blessing in disguise. The diminutive used in English, *bubeleh,* is a direct result of taking a German word for a Yiddish one.

Emergencies
There are three ways to cry for help:

geVALT	RAtevet	SHMA-yisROOel.

Gevalt can cover any contingency: accident, robbery, medical emergency, or missing the bus. *Ratevet,* literally "rescue" (think of Fontella Bass singing *"Ratevet mikh"*), is "help" in the sense of *au secours,* a cry for delivery from danger. *Shma-yisrooel* ("Hear, O Israel") are the first two words of the confession of faith found in Deuteronomy 6:4 that is recited by every orthodox Jew several times a day ("Hear, O Israel: The Lord our God, the Lord is One"); it is also supposed to be the last sentence uttered by any Jew conscious enough to know that he or she is about to die. When used to mean "help," *shma-yisrooel* implies a situation of grave and immediate danger, although it can be used ironically in situations of dubious gravity (but not by any of the principals). If your friend starts to freak out unduly over the grape juice that she's just spilled on her blouse, it's perfectly okay for *you* to say, "*Shma-yisrooel, a BLOOzeh vert geKOYlet* (Hear, O Israel, a blouse is being slaughtered)."

GEVALT

Thanks to its frequent coupling with *oy, gevalt* (sometimes transliterated as *gevald,* which reflects Yiddish spelling rather than pronunciation) is among the most popular words in the language. *Oy gevalt* can mean anything from "Heavens above" to "Oh, shit," "Fantastic," "Far freakin' out," or "I'm having an orgasm," and is probably second only to *oy vay* as the Yiddish phrase best-known to people who don't speak the language. I still treasure the memory of a friend shaking his head in wonderment and yelling, "*Gevalt,* Jimi!" after a particularly blistering solo at a 1968 Hendrix concert.

Gevalt itself means "force" or "violence"; something done *mit gevalt* is done violently or with force. *Gevalt* comes to mean "a cry for help," "a

continued...

scream," and also becomes the actual word for "cry for help." Someone yelling "*Gevalt*" can be taken as hollering "Scream!" somewhat like a character in a highly self-conscious comic; to go one step further, though, and say *gevalt* GESHRIGN, "*gevalt* has been screamed; a hue and cry is being raised" is to cross over to either the prissiness of "land sakes" or the slight vulgarity of "Jesus H. Christ."

The adjective *gevaldik* means "vast, mighty, powerful"; it's in frequent use in *frum* English to mean "great, fantastic, excellent": "She gave a *gevaldik* talk on the need for increased modesty." "He's a *gevaldik* cook."

GETTING INTO AND OUT OF TROUBLE

In cases of serious trouble, when you need urgent help of a particular kind, you can instruct the people around you as follows:

RIFT

Call—

POLITSAY	AN AMBOOLANTS	A DOKTER
the police	*an ambulance*	*a doctor.*

Other helpful phrases are:

ES BRENT, GEVALT ES BRENT!	IKH BIN NISHT SHILDIK
Fire [lit., "It's burning"]!	*I didn't do it* [lit., "I'm not guilty"].

IKH HOB ES NISHT GETEEN	IKH VIL RAIDN MIT AN AVOKAT
I didn't do it.	*I want to talk to a lawyer.*

IKH VIL RAIDN MIT AN AVOKAT VOOS RAIT YEEDEESH
I want to talk to a lawyer who speaks Yiddish.

IKH RAID NISHT KEN ENGLISH

I don't speak English.

IKH HOB AN ALERGYEH TSE

I have an allergy to—

PENITSILEEN

penicillin

STASHKES

peanuts

KHAZER

pork products

KLEZMER

klezmer music.

KHAPTS IM!

Stop, thief [lit., "Grab him, Catch him"]!

IKH HOB FARLOYREN

I've lost—

DOOS GELT

my money

DAIM BAGAZH

my baggage

DOOS BEITL

my purse or wallet

DAIM PAS

my passport

DEE ZELBST-VEERDEH

my self-respect.

LESS SERIOUS TROUBLE

IKH HOB NISH' KA' GELT

I don't have any money.

IKH BIN A YEED, IKH BIN HING'RIK, IKH HOB NISH' KA' GELT

I am a Jew, I'm hungry, I have no money.

HOST BEI ZAKH A POOR TOOLER IN KESHENEH?

Got a couple of bucks on you [lit., "in your pocket"]?

MEH ZIKHT A TSENTN

A tenth is being sought [i.e., We need someone for a minyen].

**VILST ZAKH NISHT METSAREF ZEIN? IZ ZOLST ZAKH METSAREF
ZEIN TSE AL DEE SHVARTS-YOO-ER!**

You don't want to join (the minyen)? Then you should join the devil!

*Five Little Words That Will Get You
Through Any Yiddish Conversation*

---

2. *TAKEH*

TAkeh means "really, indeed," and manages to find its way into all kinds of Yiddish sentences. Let's imagine that Esther has just explained to her skeptical tattooist that she'd like to have *kosher* inked onto the knuckles of her right hand, *traif* onto those of her left.

> ESTHER: DOOS VIL IKH TAkeh.
> *That's really what I want*

> TATTOOIST: TAkeh?
> *Really?*

> ESTHER: TAkeh.
> *Damn right.*

> TATTOOIST: EER ZENT TAkeh A KLIgeh.
> *You are really smart.*

Takeh can be used as a question in response to almost any utterance, and can be answered in turn with another *takeh,* after which it's best to revert to complete sentences (which can, however, include a *takeh*). Used judiciously by the beginner, *takeh* can help lull those around you into a belief that you've been following the conversation. ✼

3

Food and Drink

THE main problem with eating all the time is that it can get in the way of talking. Contrary to popular belief, Yiddish-speakers aren't obsessed with food; they're obsessed with talking about food, especially what's wrong with it: it's the memory of food that attracts them. Much like bores who haunt cocktail parties, telling you that they'd "like to have written, but don't like to write," the mass of Yiddish-speakers wants to have eaten far more than it really wants to eat. It's a question of satiety rather than aesthetics. Indispensable terms relating to consumption include:

TELER	SHISL	GLOOZ
plate	*bowl, dish*	*glass, cup*

A GLOOZ KAveh/TAI/MIlekh

a cup of coffee/tea/milk

GOOPL	LEFL	MEser
fork	*spoon*	*knife*

serVETkeh	TISH	TISH-TEKH
napkin	*table*	*tablecloth*

geRIKHT	MEIKHL	A BISL
dish, course	*dish, delicacy*	*a little, a bit*

NOKH A BISL

a little more

A SEEdeh FIN AKHT geRIKHTN

an eight-course meal

ZEIT ᴀ**ZOY GIT IN** ᴅᴇʀ**LANGT MEER . . .**

Please pass me . . . (polite)

GIB ᴀ**HER . . .**

Gimme here (less polite)

What you do with the stuff once you get it is pretty straightforward:

ESN	**TRINKN**	**KEI**ᴇɴ	**SHLIN**ɢᴇɴ
to eat	*to drink*	*to chew*	*to swallow*

FRESN

to gorge, eat vast amounts

SHTUPN DOOS MOYL

to stuff one's face

OONᴛʀɪɴᴋɴ **ZAKH (MIT)**

to drink one's fill, drink a lot (of)

A KHIᴅᴇsʜ **VOOS ER VERT** ᴋᴇ-**SAY**ᴅᴇʀ **GRAI**ʙᴇʀ?

Is it any wonder that he just keeps getting fatter?

ER FREST ZAKH OON A GANTSN TUG MIT ᴋʜᴀᴢᴇ**REI!**

He gorges himself on crap all day!

IN ZEE? TRINKT ZAKH OON A GANᴛsᴇʜ **NAKHT MIT BEER!**

And her? She soaks herself in beer all night!

ғᴀʀ**KHLIN**ʏᴇɴ **ZAKH**	**KRAIKN ZAKH**	**GREPSN**
to gag	*to choke*	*to belch*

GAYN IN DER LINᴋᴇʀ **KAIL** ᴀ**REIN**

to go down the wrong way [lit., "go into the windpipe"]

S'IZ MEER ᴀ**RAYN IN DER LIN**ᴋᴇʀ **KAIL**

It went down the wrong way.

SEH[ZEE/ER] KAIRT MEER BREKHN

It/she/he makes me sick; It's/she's/he's enough to make me vomit.

MEERZ ɴɪꜱʜ-GIT
I'm nauseous, I'm going to throw up.

Whoopsing Your Cookies

Like most languages whose speakers have digestive systems, Yiddish possesses more terms for human regurgitation than for human rights. Given the prominence of the upset stomach in so much Yiddish discourse, it's no surprise that the language has a full palette of expressions to describe its best-known consequence.

Heartburn, incidentally, is known as *BREɴᴇɴɪꜱʜ* or *HARTS-BREɴᴇɴ*, but these terms are used no more often than *IMꜰᴀʀDEIᴜɴɢ* and *NISHT-ꜰᴀʀDEIᴜɴɢ*, the two standard words for "indigestion," which are rarely heard in day-to-day speech. Rather than say anything, sufferers tend to clutch their chests and groan, or simply ask for *a glooz seltser.*

If none of that works, here's what happens, along with their basic meanings:

BREKHN	**ᴛꜱᴇRIKɢᴀɪʙᴍ**
to vomit	*to give back, return*
ᴋᴀPOYR SHLUGN	**GAIBM ᴋʜᴀZOOʀᴇʜ**
to bring up	*to return to sender.*

Khazooreh in the last example means "return," "repetition of a lesson," and "merchandise that has been sent back for a refund."

There's also

OYꜱᴋᴇʀɴ DEE GAL	**BREKHN MIT GREEɴᴇʜ GAL**
to pour the gall out	*to throw up green bile, vomit violently.*

Whatever comes up is known as

KAIᴇʜ	**BREKHᴇᴋʜᴛꜱ**
vomit	*vomit.*

The latter has a scarily onomatopoeic sound; fans of classical literature might notice that it also sounds a lot like the opening of the "Brekekekex" chorus in Aristophanes' *Frogs*, a fact that would undoubtedly have made Aristophanes *kvell*.

The most interesting fact about Yiddish terms for losing your lunch is their frequent association with boredom, an association not without some influence on English. The Yiddish word NOODOTEH means "nausea" or "tedium"—cause and effect are often hard to separate—and the adjective associated with it, NUDNEH, means "nauseating, boring." A *nudneh* person NUDYET—he or she bores you, forces you to endure nausea—and such a person is called a NUDNIK. English has lost the gut-wrenching physicality that Yiddish—ever mindful of its speakers' stomachs—never fails to stress; the basic meaning of *nudnik,* usually translated as "bore" or "pest," is "person who provokes vomit in another; agent of upchuck." NUDZHEN, an alternative version of *nudyen,* gives us the English noun and verb *nudge,* as in, "Quit nudging," "Don't be such a nudge"—i.e., "shut up before you make me sick to my stomach."

Praise and Blame

People who spend much of their time talking about food need a lot of words to describe it. I can't recall having ever having seen a real restaurant review in Yiddish, which tends to judge entrées by poundage and to describe most food simply as *good, better, best,* or *bad, worse, worst.* If, however, you want to get invited back to someone's house, there are some recommended terms.

The basic word for "tasty, delicious" is GESHMAK. Preceded by *der, geshmak* can also be a noun that means "taste." A dish that's really *geshmak* can be

BATAMT	A MEIKHL
tasty	*a delicacy.*

OY, IZ DOOS A MEIKHL   ES HOT A TAM-ɢᴀ-NAIDN

Oy, is this a taste-treat.   *It has the taste of paradise.*

If you say such things but don't really mean them, the food is ɪᴍ-ʙᴀTAMT—lacking in taste—but why settle for that when you can fall back on an old friend and say

ES NUDZHᴇᴛ ᴅᴇʀFIN

It makes you sick,

or

S'IZ NISHT IN MOYL TSE NAIᴍᴇɴ

You can't even get it into your mouth,

or the all-time classic,

ES HOT DER BUʙᴇs TAM

It has my grandmother's taste,

neither pleasant nor fresh.

Kosher and Nonkosher

Just about everybody knows that these are the two main categories of Jewish food. Even native Yiddish-speakers who have never kept kosher (a surprisingly large number, outside of the orthodox world) are acutely aware of the differences between kosher and nonkosher food. For speakers from more traditional backgrounds, the distinction usually remains second nature for their entire lives.

KOOsʜᴇʀ   IZ DOOS KOOsʜᴇʀ?   *DOOS* IZ KOOsʜᴇʀ?

kosher   *Is this kosher?*   This *is kosher?*

VEIZT MEER DAIM HEKHsʜᴇʀ

Show me the sign or certificate that certifies it as kosher.

DOOS IZ NISHT KEN HEKHsʜᴇʀ

This is not a hekhsher.

IKH HIT KASHᴙᴇs SHTRENG OOP, IN VAYS VER ES IZ ORVILLE REDENBACHER IN VER ES IZ A ROOV

I am fastidious in my observance of kashres *(kosherness) and can tell the difference between Orville Redenbacher and a rabbi.*

TRAIF	IKH ES NISHT KA' TRAIF	IKH ES NOR TRAIF
unkosher	*I don't eat unkosher food.*	*I only eat unkosher food.*

Important forms of non-Chinese *traif* include

KHAᴢᴇʀ	SHPEK	SHINᴋᴇʜ
pig, pork	*bacon*	*ham*

ᴋᴏʟBAS	HUZ	SHRIMP
sausage	*hare*	*shrimp.*

Gourmet *traif*:

SHTROYS	SHNEKN	ZHAʙᴇʜ-FEES
ostrich	*escargot*	*frogs' legs.*

STRICTLY KOSHER

A *hekhsher* (plural, ʜᴇᴋʜSHAIʀɪᴍ) indicates that something is kosher; it's a warrant that validates the consumption or use of a particular product by letting the consumer know that at least one rabbi has examined the raw materials and manufacturing processes and deemed them to be in accordance with the laws of Moses and Israel. If every Jew is a king or queen, then the rabbi, whose fastidiousness is all that stands between the consumer and transgression, becomes a sort of spiritual taster. Everyone who relies on a particular *hekhsher* is implicitly trusting the certifying rabbi with their lives.

Idiomatically, the idea of a farLAISlekher *hekhsher*, a reliable *heksher*, isn't restricted to rabbinic activity or things that might end up in your mouth. *Hekhsher* can be used to mean "vindication, validation, approval"; if *Good Housekeeping* were to publish in Yiddish, its famous Seal would become "*The Good Housekeeping Hekhsher*," with neither the *hekhsher* nor the seal being in any way diminished.

Despite the fact that almost every food product available in America that *can* be kosher now has a *hekhsher*, you've still got to be careful if you're planning to take food to observant friends or relatives. Never forget that the vast number of *hekhshairim* currently in existence attests to the fact that there's no such thing as absolutely kosher. *Kashres* is like beauty—it's in the eye of the person who looks but won't touch, and repudiation is the hallmark of much of what passes for Jewish observance today: the more *hekhshairim* you don't accept, the more virtuous you know yourself to be.

If you want to bring your orthodox hosts a treat, for God's sake phone first and find out what they'll eat. Ask what butcher or baker they buy from; failure to do so could earn your well-meant present a discreet trip to the garbage.

CATEGORIES OF KOSHER
Jewish law divides permitted food into three main categories:

MILkhiks	FLAYshiks	PARveh
dairy	*meat*	*neither.*

The categories are pretty straightforward, once you know that poultry is considered meat—an instance of divine grace that has kept *khayder* cafeterias chicken à la king–free since before the time of Jesus, because meat and dairy may not be eaten together. *Parveh* food—neutral food, the Switzerland of the kosher kitchen—includes fruits, vegetables, fish, and any drink without milk or cream in it.

Idiomatically, *parveh* means "nothing special, lacking any particular qualities of its own, bland." It's used more often than you might expect:

> BERL: VEE IZ geVAIN DER konTSERT?
> *How was the concert?*

> SHMERL: PARveh.
> *Nothing to write home about.*

Because you're supposed to wait six hours after eating meat before you eat any dairy, *flayshik* has come to be associated with long-lasting effects:

> NU, MAKH ZAKH FLAYshik
> *Nu, make yourself* flayshik

means, "Why don't you join me in a drink." It's the sort of invitation that implies a bottle in front of you. You can't use it to invite an object of lust or affection for a drink:

> VILST ZAKH MAKHN FLAYshik MIT MEER?
> *Wanna get* flayshik *with me?*

would make a great rhythm and blues song. It means, "Wanna fool around?" in the sense of "Why don't we give it a whirl and see where we end up?" I can still remember the kid version of Elvis's "Are You Lonesome Tonight?":

> Are you *flayshik* tonight,
> Was the *mikveh* just right?
> Are you kosher, 'cause I don't eat *traif*.

Makhn zakh flayshik is also used by people who say *nu* to drugs:

LOmeer MAKHN ZAKH FLAYshik

means, "Let's get stoned."

VILST FLAYshik VEren?

Wanna get high?

Less recreationally, a person who *makht zakh flayshik* is someone who has finally taken the plunge, as they'd say in English, and opened up a business of his or her own.

A YIDDISH VERSION OF DONNA SUMMER'S "HOT STUFF"

Kh'zits in es zakh doos harts oop, in vart meer, Vart biz a koKHAnik klingt on. OONgeDRAYT toyznt NImern shoyn, hob ikh RakhMOOnes afn teleFON.	I'm sitting here eating my heart out Waiting for a lover to call I've tried about a thousand numbers, I feel sorry for the telephone.
reFRAIN:	CHORUS:
Kh'zikh meer Epes FLAYshiks, zol meer zein YONtef. Darf ikh Epes FLAYshiks, ketsl, hei nakht, Kh'vil Epes FLAYshiks, zol meer zein YONtef	I'm looking for some *flayshiks*, let it be *yontef*, I need something *flayshik*, baby, tonight, I want something *flayshik*, let it be *yontef*

continued...

Darf ikh Epes FLAYshiks,	I need something *flayshik*,
Ersht bin ikh fin	I've just come out of the
MIKveh aROYS.	ritual bath.
Kh'darf meer FLAYshiks	I need something *flayshik*
Kh'vil Epes FLAYshiks	I want something *flayshik*
Kh'darf Epes FLAYshiks.	I need something *flayshik*.
Kh'zikh meer a koKHAnik	I'm looking for a lover
voos zikht koKHANkeh,	who wants a lover,
Nokh a nakht aLAYN	Don't want another
vil ikh nisht.	night alone
Kh'vil mesSHAmesh zein	I want to use my bed
haMEEteh vee a KAleh,	like a bride does,
Nisht tsim shlufn nor	Not for sleeping but for
tse vern geKISHT.	being kissed.
reFRAIN	CHORUS
Kh'zits in es zakh doos	I sit and eat my heart
harts imZIST oop,	out for nothing,
Nokh a nakht aLAYN vil	Don't want another
ikh nisht.	night alone.
OONgeDRAYT aHINdert	I've dialed about a
NImern shoyn, ketsl,	hundred numbers, baby,
Kayner est meer nokh nisht	But there's still nobody
daim knish.	eating my *knish*.
reFRAIN	CHORUS

Meals

A meal is known as a *MOOLtseit*. Like English, Yiddish recognizes three *mooltseitn*, along with frequent snacks:

FREEshtik	OONbeisn	VEtshereh	TSEEbeisn
breakfast	*lunch*	*supper*	*snack.*

Lunch is also known as MIteg, which is often thought of as a hot meal, as distinct from the sandwiches of *oonbeisn*. Free food is generally distributed in one of two forms:

KIbed   or   KIdesh.

Kibed, from a Hebrew word meaning "honor" or "respect," is what someone offers you if you drop by their home. It's also the snack or refreshments that follow meetings, school plays, and other such gatherings in which eating isn't the main object: "I have no interest in the organization, but they have pizza at the *kibed*," tells you a great deal about speaker and organization alike.

Kidesh, literally "sanctification," is the name for the food and drink served after a synagogue service, especially in the morning, as you're not supposed to eat before you've said your prayers. Depending on the synagogue, the time of week, and the nature of the occasion—a simple Sabbath, a bar mitzvah, a groom's prenuptial call to the Torah—it can range from depressingly meager to shockingly lavish. In the synagogues that I attended in my youth, a weekday *kidesh* usually consisted of a *shames,* a bottle and a box. A *shames* (rhymes with "pumice"), whose title gives us the English *shamus* for "private eye," is a factotum, a synagogue employee who takes care of whatever needs taking care of: setting up chairs, keeping the Torah scrolls in good repair, supervising and even leading services, teaching bar mitzvah kids, setting up the *kidesh* and cleaning up after it. Breakfast in most of the synagogues that I went to consisted of the *shames* doling out two—precisely two—Manischewitz brand Tam Tam crackers to each worshipper, while his self-appointed helper, a sort of *unter-shames,* poured each of us a shot of whiskey. On special occasions, there'd be a piece of herring, *horeh*—"no evil eye"—whenever you say anything nice. (And don't forget that you yourself could have hidden reserves of jealousy that might also need to be neutralized.) You don't want the state of being you've just described to come to a sudden end:

ZEE IZ KLIG, keNAInehoreh, VEE DRAY EINsteins
She's as smart, no evil eye, as three Einsteins

IKH FEEL ZAKH, keNAInehoreh, ZAYer GIT HEINT
I'm feeling, no evil eye, very well today.

I doubt that any amount of *kenaineh hore'ing* could save the last sentence, which has been included strictly for illustrative purposes; I've certainly never heard anything remotely like it in my life and can't imagine anyone who speaks Yiddish ever saying such a thing. More commonly, the exclamation is accompanied by a circumlocution, so that you don't actually say what it is that you're referring to. It's safer that way:

ER IZ, keNAInehoreh, NISHT KA' KAPTSN
He isn't, no evil eye, a pauper.

Any of these *kenainehorehs* can be replaced by three little spits—*ptoo ptoo ptoo*—which have the same metaphysical effect but are far more likely to spread disease on the terrestrial plane.

A BIT OF YIDDISH BABY TALK

You can teach it to your children or put on baby-doll pyjamas and pretend to be naïve. Here are a few choice specimens of real baby talk in Yiddish.

TAtesheh	**MAmesheh**
daddy	*mommy*

continued…

KOsheh	ZHOOzheh
horsie	*light, fire*

NAM-NAM

food (Remember Peter Sellers in *The Party?*)

HAM	HAMenyoo	HAmen
food	*food (diminutive)*	*to eat*

HEIteh	GAYN HEIteh
walk	*to go for a walk*

Other Necessary Exclamations

No Yiddish conversation would be complete without at least a couple of hollered phrases; if nothing else, they help to keep everybody awake. The best known is

MAZL TOV

Congratulations.

Don't hesitate to use it ironically.

Less good-natured but considerably more useful is

A BROKH

or more commonly,

OY, A BROKH

Oh hell, oh damn, oh shit [lit., "a break, a fracture; a misfortune"].

There's also the highly versatile

A KLUG.

Literally "a lament, a complaint," *klug* is extremely versatile (the official Yiddish word for complain is BaKLUGN zakh; if you want to call another kid a crybaby, KLUGmiter—roughly, *mater lacrimosa*, "wailing woman, professional mourner"—is probably your best bet).

On its own as above, it's roughly equivalent to *a brokh*—possibly a little less rude. Rather than "oh shit," it's probably closer to "Good God!" or, to stretch an idiom, the kind of "Jesus Christ!" that comes out of your mouth after you've hit your thumb with a hammer.

A KLUG TSE IM/EER
Screw him/her.

Think of Eric Cartman on *South Park:*

A KLUG TSE EIKH ALEmen, IKH GAY aHAYM
Screw you guys, I'm going home.

When the *klug* is yours, though, everything's different:

A KLUG TSE MEER
Oy vay; alas; woe is me.

This sort of reversal is seen at its best with a fabulous pair of expressions that use the word YOOR, "year."

aZA YOOR AF MEER
Such a year on me

means "it should happen to me," as in:

ER HOT GeKROGN DEE NoBEL PREMyeh? aZA YOOR AF MEER
He won the Nobel Prize? It should only happen to me.

In the second or third persons, though, it means "it should happen to you (because I don't like you and would enjoy seeing you suffer)":

ZEE IZ IMgefaln IN tseBRUKHN A FEES? AZA YOOR AF DEER
She fell down and broke her leg? It should only happen to you.

And, returning to *klug*, let's not forget the indispensable:

VOOS IZ MIT IM DER KLUG?
What the hell/what the fuck is wrong with him?

or more colloquially these days, *What's his problem?*

There are also any number of substitutes that can be used for the rather tired *oy vay*. All of them mean *oy vay*, but they help keep the suffering spicy:

OKH	OKH IN VAY	VAY IZ MEER
OKH IN VAY TSE MEER	VAY geSHRIGN	

A really nice touch can be achieved by using the phrase *SOYneh-TSEE-yen*, "enemies of Zion." The anti-Semites are invoked along with the mention of something horrible, as if to say, may the calamity herein described befall the enemies of Israel rather than any of us. Here is a quotation from the beginning of the first of Sholem Aleykhem's Tevye stories, followed by an example of our own:

KHOTSH NEM LAYG ZAKH, SOYneh-TSEE-yen, IN SHTARB
You might as well lie down, enemies of Zion, and die.

SEH HOT ZAKH geTROFN A SHREKlakh IMglik, SOYneh TSEE-yen
There was a horrible accident, enemies of Zion.

Soyneh tseeyen is a more aggressive version of *nisht far ken yeedn gedakht*, "it shouldn't happen to a Jew."

Another pair of intensifiers, no longer used as often as they should be, is *saKOOnes*, "dangers," and its close relative *saKOOnes-neFOOshes*, "danger to life, deadly peril." Each means "very much, terribly":

ZEE IZ farLEEBT IN IM saKOOnes/saKOOnes-neFOOshes
She's head over heels in love with him.

Finally, there's the monosyllable of universal disapprobation that can be used to describe anything that fails to meet your approval—food, a smell, a movie, a book, an opinion, a person, a person's appearance, a date, a car, an ideology, and so on:

FEH.

It means: "It stinks." It is not to be confused with its near relative

FNYEH,

which means "nothing special, so-so," but tending toward the wrong "so." If someone asks:

VEE IZ geVAIN DER FILM?

How was the movie?

and you respond with

FNYEH,

you're saying that while it might not have stunk, it was certainly no rose. What it was, is *parveh*—not terribly good, not even terribly bad, with a slight but unmistakably unpleasant aftertaste. Better than a trip to the dentist, but not so good that you'd hate yourself for dozing off at the climax.

NONE TOO BRIGHT

Yiddish is blessed with a wealth of expressions to describe anybody less intelligent than the speaker. Some of the best are:

ER VAYST NISHT FIN DEE HENT MIT DEE FEES
He doesn't know from his hands or his feet; doesn't know shit from shinola

continued...

ZEE HOT aZOY FEEL SAYKHL VEE IN KLOYster meZIzes
She has as many brains as a church has mezuzas

SEH FELT EER MAIBL IN BOYdem-SHTEEBL
She's got no furniture in her attic

KHOTSH NEM IN MELK IM
You might as well milk him, [i.e., he's a beHAYmeh—a cow, a beast, an idiot].

DEFENSE MECHANISMS

Feh and *fnyeh* are usually accompanied by a dismissive wave of the hand intended to indicate that

SHAInereh LAYGT MEN IN DR'ERD aREIN

Better-looking specimens of the same thing are laid in the ground,

i.e., you've seen corpses that were less carcasslike. The wrist, generally the right, bends until the fingertips are parallel to the floor, but only after the whole arm, starting from the shoulder, has been moved far enough to the left to bring the crook of the right elbow into line with your nose at precisely the second when the wrist goes down—as if you were removing whatever you're talking about from your presence, if not actually forcing it into the grave that it really deserves. This highly physical farewell to any dignity that might still be clinging to the object of your scorn is characterized as

aVEKmakhn MIT DER HANT

to remove or set at a distance by means of the hand

The thing in question is so slight and insubstantial that the merest wave of the hand is enough to send it packing. Hence the more idiomatic English rendering, "to brush off, shrug off." Someone who

MAKHT Epes aVEK MIT DER HANT

is usually ignoring warnings based on the experiences of others or severely underestimating whatever is being dismissed so cavalierly.

"RAK, SHMAK!" ER FLAIGT aVEKmakhn DEE geFARN FIN RAYkhern MIT DER HANT

"Cancer, shmancer!" He used to shrug off the dangers of smoking

and, it is understood, is now paying the price for having done so.

Avekmakhn mit der hant can also be used of someone who's downplaying an achievement of their own, whether it's the help they gave you when you really needed it or the Nobel Prize that they've just been awarded. In such cases the *makh*—the swing, stroke or wave—usually goes along with *aderabeh* or *s'iz nisht*, the equivalents of "Shucks, 'twarn't nothing," that we saw on page 24.

Both usages display a certain contempt for the activity under consideration, a contempt that links the idea of *avekmakhn mit der hant* to family life and conversation. As the sole emotion that many Yiddish-speakers feel comfortable about expressing, contempt—especially that of age for youth and youth for age—plays an unusually prominent role in Yiddish domestic discourse.

Yiddish-speakers are rarely jealous of their children, because they—the parents—are so much smarter than the kids that it isn't even funny. HisKATnoo ha-DOYres, the generations have grown smaller, as the saying has it; each successive generation is more remote from the revelation at Mount Sinai, a little farther away from the source of ultimate wisdom. Ever since Moses, we've been shrinking. Your *tateh* and *mameh* might not be much, but they're still older than you are, still closer to Sinai, a fact of which they're never slow to remind you. Since you're so much younger, you can't ever be expected to grasp this state of affairs; you're condemned to continue your unconscious assault on the dignity of your elders until they go on to a better place and you begin to notice how far short of the mark anyone born after you falls:

MOYsheh raBAYnee? MEIN ELter-ZAYdeh FIN MAmens TSAD HOT
GeKENT YEEDN VOOS ZEnen geZESN MIT IM IN AYN KHAYder

*Moses our teacher? My maternal great-grandfather knew people
who went to Hebrew school with him.*

This attitude of being endowed with a dollop more of the spirit of wisdom by virtue of having been born before you got old manifests itself in three major conversational attitudes: offense, contempt, and disparagement.

OFFENSE

It's the root of all *kvetching*. It's no good if they ignore you; it's worse if they look too closely. Either nobody listens to anything you say or else no one has the brains to make the simplest decision without coming to you. If you're indispensable, they're working you to death; if you're not, they don't appreciate you. In either case, you can always make use of a good "What am I?"

"What am I?" transforms a rhetorical question into a kind of conversational parlor-game that places a single active player—you—in front of a roomful of losers-by-definition who are powerless to do anything but hem and haw with increasing discomfort as you ask question after question that cannot be answered. Remember, the bolder the metaphor, the more extreme the comparison, the smaller the chance of anyone being able to respond. Whoever starts the game, wins.

If you're being *nudged* to death, try

VOOS BIN IKH DEN . . .

So what am I . . .

and then add the appropriate follow-up. *Den* is a highly useful particle that turns a question from something to be answered into something to be feared. A plain question like "What am I, an asshole?" could get you an affirmative response. "What am I *den,* an asshole?" lets everybody know that the answer is no and that they don't need to bother telling you so.

VOOS BIN IKH DEN, AN AIᴠᴇᴅ-ᴋ'NAɴᴇʜ?

What am I, a Canaanite slave?

Unlike an Israelite slave, a Canaanite slave was a slave forever and lived without much hope of being released. He was also unlikely to speak much Yiddish. The phrase means "Ask someone else for a change."

If someone is trying to dupe you or pull the wool over your eyes, you can change the second part of the question—the *zets,* "the blow, the thump, the punch line"—to *a nekhtiker* and say:

VOOS BIN IKH DEN, A NEKHᴛɪᴋᴇʀ?

What am I, born yesterday?

Nekhtiker is an adjectival form of *nekhtn,* "yesterday," and means "belonging to or having to do with yesterday, with times past." Should you describe somebody as being *like* a *nekhtiker,* though, you're basically saying that they're at a psychic impasse, full of confusion and anomie:

ER IZ VEE A NEKHᴛɪᴋᴇʀ

means that he's sad, confused, depressed, and therefore as dull and lifeless as yesterday is today. Similarly,

A NEKHtiker TUG

a yesterday's day

means "Tell it to the marines ('cause there's nobody here who's going to listen)."

While we're talking about marines, it's worth noting that in his 1928 *Yiddish-English-Hebrew Dictionary*, Alexander Harkavy actually goes so far as to gloss

derTSAYL ES DER BUben

Tell it to your granny

as "tell it to the marines," despite the fact that no Yiddish-speaking Jew ever tells a marine *anything*: he's too busy running in the other direction. Even though there is an episode of *Gomer Pyle, U.S.M.C.* in which Molly Picon—a veritable Yiddish superstar—plays a lonely Jewish *bubeh* living in a trailer near Gomer's base, dispensing heartache and advice in equal measures, *Gomer Pyle* is not an entirely accurate mirror of the American Jewish experience.

Similar in meaning to *nekhtiker* but edgier (and a lot smarter sounding) is

VOOS BIN IKH DEN, Epes A YUsem KUTN?

What am I, an orphan toddler?

born yesterday and with no one to show you the ropes? The *epes* here adds the right note of contempt—"some kind of," as if you can't even be credited with having the brains to know what you really are.

If you feel that you're being ignored or overlooked, you can ask indignantly:

VOOS BIN IKH DEN, AN OOnee ba-PEsakh

What am I, a beggar at your door,

forced to beg for what is mine by rights and hope that you'll do me a favor and let me have it? It's a powerful image, drawn from the

Rosh Hashana liturgy: "I come before You to beg for mercy like a beggar in Your doorway." If Tony Bennett had recorded "Rags to Riches" in Yiddish, "Must I forever be a beggar / Whose golden dreams will not come true" would have come out as "*Miz ikh ke-oonee shtayn ba-pesakh/Mit khaLOYmes AYbik pist.*"

If you're *really* angry about being treated so badly, if they've behaved as if you weren't even there, you can throw in a surprise direct question and ask,

> *IKH* HOB ZAKH GeSHMAT?
>
> I *converted to Christianity?*

Does that explain why I don't figure in the quorum of those who matter?

While the question about conversion follows nicely from a rhetorical question, it is generally more effective when used on its own, especially if you refer to yourself in the third person as if you were talking, dispassionately, of an offer or invitation to some arm's-length third party whose presence would only—or so you think—enhance the enterprise in question and make it even more successful:

> NU . . .

This *nu* must be uttered as if the idea had just occurred to you:

> NU, VEKS HOT ZAKH OOPGeSHMAT?
>
> *Has Wex taken a dip in the baptismal font?*

as if to say, "There is only one possible reason why the name that I'm about to mention has not been raised thus far" (*oopgeshmat* is a more intensive form of *geshmat*).

If you've not only been overlooked or passed over, but also have to listen to an unending stream of praise for the person who got whatever should have been yours, you can show just how sick you are of hearing about her—or anybody else who is being implicitly compared with you to your detriment—by saying,

> VOOS BIN IKH DEN, A kaPOOreh FAR EER FOO-erts?
> *What am I, an atonement for her fart?*

How will hurting *me* bring her closer to perfection?

CONTEMPT

If they haven't got the idea by this point, they're unlikely to get it at all. But if we could leave well enough alone, we'd never have got ourselves into the metaphysical mess that led to the development of Yiddish, so go ahead and tell them explicitly that whoever you're talking about

> IZ NISHT VERT AN OYSgebloozn AY
> *isn't worth a blown-out egg,*

compared to you, they're nothing but a hound dog. When it comes to crooning,

> FRENK seNAtreh IZ A HINT KAIGN MEER
> *Frank Sinatra is a dog compared to me,*

> IKH KEN IM farSHTEKN IN MEIN GARTL
> *I can stick him in the sash I wear while praying*

because he doesn't even come up to my baby finger.

The most useful way of expressing contempt for almost anything is probably

> OYKH MEER A . . .

It means "some . . . , what a . . ."

OYKH MEER A ZINGer	OYKH MEER A KEEkher
Some singer	*Some cook*

Winston Churchill's secret Yiddish speech to the Canadian Senate on December 30, 1941, concludes with:

OYKH MEER A HINDL; OYKH MEER A HELDZL

Some chicken; some neck

The basic meaning of *oykh meer a . . .* is "[this], too, [should be considered] by me a . . . ," as in, "I should consider *this* to be a chicken or a neck? Never!"

If everybody else is going wild for something about which you're saying *oykh mir a,* you'll ask:

VOOS IZ DEE GDIleh?

What's the big deal?

VOOS MAKHT MEN aZA hoo-HAH?

What's all the hullabaloo?

Hoo-hah is a rather cruel expression that can be used to

MAKHN ASH IN BLOOteh

make ash and mud

out of just about anything; it is about as irreversible as Yiddish gets and, as such, should not be used lightly. Imagine a deadpan, patently insincere declaration of "Oh, joy," multiplied to the power of ten. *Hoo-hah*—which doesn't *have* to be used ironically, but almost always is—can knock the life out of anything. It's "Oh, joy" with a blunt instrument in its hand:

YOU: TAtesheh, TAtesheh, IKH HOB HEINT geVINen DREI OSkers.

Daddy, Daddy, I won three Oscars today.

DAD: hoo-HAH! VOOS MEH PLAIT HEINT NISHT OYS!

Hoo-hah! What they don't *raffle off these days!*

Have the limo go straight to your therapist's.

Once something's been *hoo-hahed*, it's as good as dead and can't be brought back to life until the Messiah arrives. Best, then, to stick to *gdileh*, and if that isn't enough on its own, stave off the fatal *hoo-hah* with

A GDILeh AF DEIN BUben

a gdileh on your granny [i.e., *nothing much to boast about*].

Grandmothers take up a lot of room in Yiddish put-downs, and the *bubehs gdileh*, the grandmother's glory, sometimes appears in more baroque form as

A GDILeh—DEE BUbeh HOT KHAseneh geHAT!

Great day in the morning! Granny got married!

The point of the joke resides in the fact that traditionally the real *gdileh* consists of marrying off your youngest daughter—at one time the final barrier to being able to live for yourself instead of your children, since no dowry had to be furnished for even the *zhlobiest* of sons.

The same *bubeh* also appears in

MEIN BUbehs DEIgeh

My grandmother's worry,

which means that it's no worry of mine, as does

OYKH MEER A DEIgeh

some worry,

which is virtually synonymous with

A DEIgeh MEIneh

a worry of mine,

which means no worry of mine at all.

A pointless worry, something not worth losing even a second's worth of sleep over, can be dismissed in one word as

BLOOᴛᴇʜ

mud,

probably better rendered in this context as "crap." It can also be used to mean even less:

S'IZ BLOOᴛᴇʜ

It's nothing,

no more important or valuable than the mud that we scrape off our shoes. *Blooteh* is also used as a purely categorical exclamation, a nearly automatic response to any crap that you happen to hear:

THEM: CURLY JOE IZ ɢᴇVAIN BEsᴇʀ FIN CURLY.
Curly Joe was better than Curly.

YOU: BLOOᴛᴇʜ!
Bullshit!

Contempt for bullshit gives us one of the most remarkable, not to mention useful, phrases in the language:

VAYS IKH VOOS

(lit., "I know what;" more literally, "know I what")

Uriel Weinreich, in his *Modern English-Yiddish Yiddish-English Dictionary* translates it as "tut! pooh! nonsense! fiddlesticks!" all of which are perfectly correct. They are not, however, entirely idiomatic:

DESPERATE JUNKIE: *A YN* ZEᴋᴇʟᴇʜ, GIB MEER NOR *A YN* ZEᴋᴇʟᴇʜ.
MEIN TSHEK KIMT MORGN OON.
One bag, just gimme one bag. My check will be here tomorrow.

HEARTLESS PUSHER: VAYS IKH VOOS!
Fiddlesticks!

Even in the less B-movie circumstances (perhaps it's best to say *other* B-movie circumstances) in which most Yiddish-speakers do their Yiddish-speaking, *vays ikh voos* has an air of contempt that is positively menacing—to your interlocutor's self-regard, if nothing else. It's never pronounced as clearly as it's written here; it is spat—ideally, it's *sneezed* out, slow-roasted over the adenoids before being projected through the nose, and sounds more like VEI-KH-OO-EHS than a series of separate words. Rather than "tell it to the marines," *vays ikh voos* is closer to "For this"—the crap that you've just heard—"For this God gave you a mouth?!" It consists of equal parts disbelief, contempt, and impatience—practically a Yiddish trifecta. While not recommended for telephone use—people are likely to say "Gesundheit" or ask if you're all right—it's perfect for dealing with any idiot separated from you by a counter or desk (so long as they aren't wearing judge's robes); the air of bubbling menace will get them even if they don't understand a word.

JESUS CHRIST

Years ago, I was watching television with my maternal grandmother when a commercial sponsored by one or another of the "Jesus is the reason for the season" Christian groups came on. As the commercial came to a close, the announcer on the voiceover solemnly said, "For God so loved the world that He gave his only son, that whoever believes in Him should not perish but have eternal life," to which my *bubeh,* a gifted amateur theologian who loved nothing better than to talk back to her television, replied:

VAYS IKH VOOS! 'KH ZOL BEser GLAYBM IN YOSHkeh PANdreh!
bull-SHIT! I'd go for Jesus before I'd go for that!

With respect to something—Jesus, sports scores, the troubles of others—that don't make you no never mind, you can say:

MIKH ARTS NISHT

It doesn't concern me/doesn't matter to me; I don't care.

You can make it more Yiddish by putting it in the form of a question that would yell at any attempted answer:

VOOS ART MIKH?

What do I care?

MIKH ART DEN Epes?

What's it to me?

Only you are allowed to answer these, and you can do so by saying,

S'ART MIKH VEE DER faraYOOriker SHNAY

I'm as worried about it as I am about last year's snow [or *les neiges d'antan,*
if you're in a more wistful mood]

Nonsense, trifles, pointless crapola of the type that couldn't possibly interest you is called

SHMONtses	**SHMOKHtehs**
nonsense, idle talk	*trifles, nonsense*
shaleMOYZN	**zabaBOnehs**
whims, nonsense	*nonsense, delusions.*

Such matters are so foolish that

luBAvitcher LAKHN derFIN

[*even*] *Lubavitcher hasidim laugh at them.*

This is a fairly recent addition to the canon. I heard it in an orthodox synagogue in the fall of 2005, about ten seconds after some visiting scholar or other had proclaimed Hurricane Katrina to be God's judgment on the minor-league Sodom that calls itself New Orleans. The man who blurted it out admitted to having modeled it on the well-known and much older

KHSIᴅɪᴍ LAKHN ᴅᴇʀFIN

hasidim laugh at it (i.e., *even the most credulous of the credulous can't take it seriously*),

an expression still current during his youth in Europe.

DISPARAGEMENT

Uttered in the proper tone of voice, virtually any phrase in this book can be turned into an insult. True, no great imagination is needed to see how something like *mazl tov* can be used to "congratulate" someone who has ignored previous results and repeated an oft-repeated mistake, or gone ahead and done something after multiple warnings not to. Yiddish might embrace such low-level irony, but it also goes far beyond it. Apparently innocent statements, fact-delivery systems that are supposed to have as little to do with emotion or opinion as mezuzahs do with mezzotints, can be turned into *shpilkes*, pins, to be used as agents of deflation. *Shpilkes* are well-known from such phrases as:

IKH ZITS AF SHPILᴋᴇꜱ

I'm on pins and needles; I can't wait; I've got ants in my pants.

The English version, "I've got *shpilkes*"—as if *shpilkes* were rhythm—doesn't work for anyone who already speaks Yiddish. *Everybody* has nonmetaphorical *shpilkes,* and in the days before Velcro, *shpilkes,* in the form of diaper pins, were the first fashion accessory worn by most human beings. If you say "I've got *shpilkes*" rather than "I'm on *shpilkes*" or "sitting on *shpilkes,*" you'd best add "in my posterior" to those pins if you want to make any real sense.

Shpilkes can penetrate; they can prick egos as well as fingers, burst all your hopes and dreams and claim to do so out of love: "We didn't want you to be disappointed if things didn't work out." It's the domestic interpretation of the rabbinic maxim, "Know what is above you" (Ovos, 2:1). Where the sages meant that God was watching, the rest of the Jews take it to mean "Don't get too big for your britches: given the nature of the world around us, we believe in the near inevitability of failure and we're doing this out of love." So when you say, "Mom, Dad, I'm quitting med school to devote myself to playing the koto," the first thing they'll do is remind you of what you've just said by repeating the name of the activity that you've mentioned:

VEST SHPEELN KOTO?

You're going to play the koto?

Then they'll answer themselves:

VEST SHPEELN *KO*TO.

You're going to play the koto.

And then, with head turned to the side, whether anybody else is there or not, they'll ask another question:

HERST?

You hear?

ER VIL SHPEELN KOTO NOKH.

He wants to play the koto, yet.

The *herst* in the third line is vital here and is especially effective when only two people are present. The appeal to an invisible force—the ambient Jewish mind, a tribunal of the world's super-egos, the ear of God implied by the Mishna—the constant wondering if people who aren't there have heard and absorbed the fullness of your folly, is really an attempt to save you from your-self, to spare you the trouble of having to justify your idiocy on that great and terrible day of judgment that non-Yiddish-speakers describe as "maybe not today, maybe not tomorrow, but soon, and for the rest of your life":

EFsher NISHT HEINT, EFsher NISHT MORGN, NOR BALD, IN
BIZ NOKH HINdert IN TSVONtsik YOOR.

Casablanca is a film with a marked Yiddish influence, pro-foundly touched by Yiddish turns of phrase and patterns of speech: "Of all the gin joints in all the towns all over the world, she walks into mine," follows the very rhythms of Yiddish speech—it sure doesn't help to make Humphrey Bogart sound like the ex-gunrunner that he's supposed to be. In real Yiddish, though, we're all supposed to make like Ingrid Bergman and let someone else do the thinking. In real Yiddish the problems of "three little people"—even two little people—far from not amounting "to a hill o' beans in this crazy world," are really *all* that matters—at least for the next ninety seconds. So go ahead, play it, Sam—and let me point out your mistakes.

But how? With what *shpilkeh* can I burst your balloons full of hope? With damned near any word in the language, with almost any of the words and phrases listed in this book. Yiddish might well be unique in its ability to turn almost any noun into a term of opprobrium; Sholem Aleykhem's page-and-a-half-long alphabet-ical list of insults hurled at him by his stepmother includes such terms as pauper, broom, squirrel, sack, hidden saint, limping tailor, gentile girl, epileptic, belly-button, synagogue orator, hatmaker, and potato eater. I myself was called athlete, money-maker, and—the one that really lingers—air conditioner, at various times in my youth. So just close this book, reopen it, and choose a phrase at random. Let's see: Page 24?

VILST SHPEELN KOᴛᴏ? ZOL ES DEER VOYL ʙᴀKIᴍᴇɴ

You want to play koto? Many happy returns [i.e., *I hope you
and your koto are very happy together*].

Should you open to page 53, which is full of names for kitchen utensils? *Nu?*

VILST SHPEELN KOTO? DEE BIST A TISH-TEKH

You want to play koto? You're a tablecloth.

Or page 189?

KOTO? ᴀVEE IZ DER ᴋʟᴏZET?

Koto? Where's the toilet?

And just to prove the point, let's try the entirely positive page 23 and what do we find?

VILST SHPEELN Koᴛᴏ? YᴀsʜᴇR KOYᴇᴋʜ! *IKH* VIL SHPEELN A ᴅᴏᴏET MIT
MERʟɪɴ ᴍᴏɴRO

*You wanna play the koto? More power to you! I wanna play a duet
with Marilyn Monroe.*

There's a proverb that says *a vort iz vee a feil,* a word is like an arrow: it doesn't take long to penetrate.

It Can't Hurt

Sometimes, though, a Yiddish-speaker runs across something really impressive, something so undeniably amazing that he or she *wants* to appreciate it for what it is. Such a thing—a wonder of nature, a work of art, a tasty dessert—can be described as

ɢᴇVALᴅɪᴋ	MERKᴠᴇRᴅɪᴋ
mighty, powerful; excellent	*remarkable.*

An especially good example of something can be described as an *X* from *X*-land. A great book, for instance is

A BEEKH FIN BEEKHᴇʀʟᴀɴᴛ
a book from bookland.

A table is

A TISH FIN TISHNʟᴀɴᴛ
a table from the land of tables.

A piece of matzoh would be

A MAᴛsᴇʜ FIN MAᴛsᴇʟᴀɴᴛ

and a *real* Jew, as distinct from total fakes and ersatz Jews made of chicory—the kind that Yiddish-speakers are always running into—is called

A YEED FIN YEEDNʟᴀɴᴛ.

If you're admiring the way that somebody does something, you can use the phrase *doos hayst* followed by the past participle of the verb that describes the activity:

DOOS HAYST ɢᴇZINɢᴇɴ
Now that's singing/That's what I call singing.

If you should tell a friend that the people in the next room kept you up all night in your hotel, your friend might say,

THEM: A GANᴛsᴇʜ NAKHT ɢᴇPREIKHT IN ɢᴇSHRIGN?
A whole night of panting and screaming?

NU, DOOS HAYST ɢᴇSHMINTST.
Nu, that's what I call screwing.

YOU: YEH, ZAY HOBM ɢᴇSHMINTST ʙᴇʜ-TAKHʟɪs ha-SHMINTSN.
Yeah, they were well and truly screwing.

To do anything *be-takhlis ha-(fill in the blank)* is to do it to the utmost or utterly or extremely. *Er curlt be-takhlis ha-curling* would mean "he does extreme curling." The idiom's most common use is probably in the phrase

FEINT HOBM be-TAKHlis ha-SEEneh

to loathe, hate implacably.

TAKHLIS

Be-takhlis is derived from the very prominent Yiddish noun, *takhlis*, which is among the most useful and versatile words in the language. Of Hebraic origin, *takhlis* has a fundamental meaning of "result, practical purpose; the end or aim of an activity," and therefore, "serious business of the sort to which you get down."

LOmeer RAIDN FIN TAKHlis
Let's talk takhlis

is the Yiddish counterpart of talking turkey. It means "let's get to the real purpose of all this talk," which usually (although not always) means "let's talk practical arrangements and—even more important—money." This use of *takhlis* is closely related to the one found in

ZIKHN A TAKHlis
to look for a takhlis,

which means "to look for a way to earn a living, to try to find some sort of work or occupation."

The very common

VOOS IZ DER TAKHlis?
What's the takhlis?

often translated as "what's the use; what's the point; why bother?" has a more literal meaning of "What's the end going to be? What's going to

continued...

result from this?" The more usual English translation merely assumes the almost inevitably negative response.

MAKHN A TAKHLIS FIN
To make a takhlis *of*

the means and opportunities at your disposal means that you've put them to good purpose, or alternatively—and it should come as no surprise— you've reduced them to nothing, destroyed them completely:

ZEE HOT GEMAKHT A TAKHLIS FIN EER TATENS GESHEFT

means either

> *"She made good use of her father's business, put it to good purpose"*

or

> *"She destroyed her father's business for good and all."*

If you see or experience something really incredible—regardless of whether it is positive or negative—you can say,

ES IZ NISHT TSE GLAYBM
It's unbelievable, incredible [lit., "not to be believed"].

Der kontsert iz nisht gevain tse glaybm tells you that the concert was incredible, just as *Eer khitspeh iz nisht tse glaybm* tells you the same thing about her chutzpah.

A new and better way of doing something, or a technological marvel, a gadget, a doo-hickey, a whizzbang or rocket-to-the-moon that can shine your shoes, whistle "Dixie" and *daven minkheh* while doing your taxes in the time that it takes to swallow three raw eggs in rapid succession is worthy of the once common and now unquestionably revival-worthy

aMErikeh GAnef.

The literal meaning of *ganef* is "thief"; in some contexts, though, it also takes on a sense of "clever fellow who does things in an unconventional way that might involve subtle reinterpretation of the usual rules." Had they only existed, the Yiddish-speakers present when Alexander the Great untied the Gordian knot by cutting it with his sword would have exclaimed, *"Alexander ganef!"*

Amerikeh ganef implies an affectionate, somewhat admiring bemusement at the antics of America, here portrayed as a clever, slightly mischievous young scamp of a country, the national version of a

MAzik	SHTIfer	KINdehs
little devil, rascal	*scalawag, scamp*	*prankster, mischief maker*

or even a

SHAYgets
young gentile; [of a Jew] *wise ass, smart aleck,*
maker of monkey business.

Monkey business, pranks, and the like are known in Yiddish as

SHMAD-SHTIK
apostasy shtik,

shtik so wild that you wouldn't have expected it of a Jew—the premise of Sacha Baron Cohen's Borat is a series of *shmad–shtik*. While *shmad–shtik* is not usually used as a compliment, any of the nouns just listed can be used to express approval, if not outright admiration. They are the real Yiddish for what English now calls "a person with plenty of chutzpah." Chutzpah, or KHITSpeh in the dialect that we're using, is never a good thing in Yiddish. *Khitspeh* involves an offensive disregard for manners, social conventions, or the feelings of others, and is rooted in a kind of solipsism that won't acknowledge anyone but oneself as completely real. In Yiddish, a clever, nervy person will be called a *mazik* or a MAMzer—a bastard—and people will talk about his *saykhl*, his intelligence or brains. *Khitspeh* consists of visiting someone's home and taking a dump in their potted plant; *saykhl* is taking the same dump in a field and using it for fertilizer. Should you ever be confused or stumble onto the occasional gray area between *khitspeh* and *saykhl*, just ask yourself if it's pissed you off: in Yiddish, there's no *khitspeh* without anger.

Negative amazement of the type embodied in *khitspeh* is usually underlined by

TSEITN derLAIBT!

The times that we've lived to see!

The Yiddish equivalent of Cicero's *"O tempora! O mores," tseitn derlaibt* can be used to express astonished admiration, but is more usually heard in exclamations of dismay. In the latter sense, it's very much part of the whole *hiskatnoo ha-doyres* mentality, the idea that each new generation is weaker than the last, and is best regarded as another testimony to the continuing decline of human character.

Its close associate

meSHEE-ekhs TSEITN!

The messianic era! The millennium! The rapture is here!

is generally used as a somewhat mocking description of an action, laudable enough on its own, but performed by someone who would never normally be expected to do such a thing. Macy shaking hands with Gimble in *Miracle on 34th Street* is a *locus classicus* for the use of such an expression, as is your adolescent child's making the bed of his or her own volition when there is no bad news on the way. In such cases, *tseitn derlaibt* could also be used; it would, however, be overtly insulting—best translated as

"Look what finally got off its ass"—where *meshee-ekhs tseitn* conveys a pleasantly surprised bemusement.

Any truly amazing sight—Vesuvius in eruption, a UFO landing, that teenager making the bed—can be described as a

BAYZ-VINDER

a stone marvel, a freak of friggin' nature.

Despite its large number of meanings, *bayz* doesn't really mean either "stone" or "freak." Its senses cover a range of unpleasantness that goes from "bad, evil, wicked," through "angry, ill-disposed, indignant," to "severe, fierce," and "wrong." *Bayz* can provide a handy guide to Yiddish conversation almost entirely on its own. If the Hippocratic oath really started with, "First, do no harm," the Yiddish version would be

RAIshis KOL, TIT NISHT KEN BAYZ

First, do no harm.

We've already seen *bayz* in this sense of "harm, evil" in connection with the *bayz oyg,* the evil eye, discussed above. The same meaning also comes up in the rather discomfiting

A BAYzeh SHOO

an evil or *ill-starred hour.*

This is the opposite of the good and auspicious hour that is often added to wishes of *mazl tov:*

MAZL TOV! ZOL ZEIN IN A GIter IN A MAZLdiker SHOO

Mazl tov! May it take place in a good and auspicious hour.

A *mazl* is a constellation or sign of the zodiac; the congratulations above express a wish that the stars be lined up in a way that is favorable to the success of the enterprise. The *bayzeh shoo* describes the idea expressed in the Prologue to *Romeo and Juliet:*

A POOR geLEEBteh IN A BAYzer SHOO
A pair of star-crossed lovers.

The events of the *bayzeh shoo* can be described as

A BAYZ YOOR
disaster, calamity [lit., "an evil year"],

the sort of thing that you wish on someone who has wronged you, your friends and family, the whole of the Jewish people and most of the rest of humanity:

A BAYZ YOOR AF IM
May a disaster befall him.

Calamity Jane would have been called *Jane Bayz-Yoor* in Yiddish.

Such calamities and disasters tend to be the topics of a BAYZEH PSEEreh, bad news or evil tidings:

DER VOOS LAKHT HOT NOKH NISHT geHERT DEE BAYzeh PSEEreh,

as Bertolt Brecht once said in another language: "He who laughs has not yet heard the bad news."

Bayzeh pseereh is a demi-translation of the completely Hebraic PSEEREH ROO'eh, which means exactly the same thing. Their antonyms, GIteh pseereh and pseereh TOYveh, are both reflections of the Hebrew *besoyroh toyvoh*, "good tiding, good news," which is also the ultimate source of the Greek *euangelion*, the good news that announces the arrival of Christ and gives us such words as "evangelist." It's the Yiddish way: when the good news is Jesus, all *pseerehs* are *bayz*.

This use of *bayz* as the Germanic counterpart of the Hebrew *rah*, which has a very similar range of meaning, pops up again with BAYZEH KHEIyeh, the fierce or wild beast first found in Genesis 37, where Joseph's brothers put it about that "a *khayoh ro'oh*, a wild beast, has devoured him." While *bayzeh kheiyeh* doesn't tend to come up very often in day-to-day Yiddish, a more direct translation of the same Hebrew phrase has long been indispensable wherever parents and Yiddish meet:

VOOS LOYFstee IM VEE A VILdeh KHEIyeh?
What are you running around like a wild animal for?

HEINtikeh KINder FEErn ZAKH VEE VILdeh KHEIyehs
Kids today behave like wild animals.

Vildeh kheiyehs bug their parents; *bayzeh khayehs* eat them. Either can provoke a situation that leads to a parent becoming angry.

ZEIN BAYZ
to be angry

is pretty much the same as a number of other idioms relating to anger.

ER IZ BAYZ AF MEER
He's mad at me

means exactly the same thing as

ER BAYzert ZAKH AF MEER
he's mad at me; also, he's bawling me out.

Being *bayz* isn't the same as doing *bayz,* though:

ER HOT EER BAYZ geTEEN
He done her wrong

can also mean that he harmed her. Whoever he is, he's

A BAYZer MENTSH
wicked, angry; stern and unfriendly;

to change sex for a moment, he's Elvira Gulch.

Finally, there's the incredibly useful idiom

MIT BAYZN

against one's will; with severity; by means of threats; by force,

the way most *vildeh kheiyeh* children do most things demanded of them by their parents. *Mit bayzn* also helps get us to the very common

MIT GITN TSEE MIT BAYZN

by any means necessary; "by hook or crook" [Uriel Weinreich];
"one way or another" [Deborah Harry].

Mit gitn means "of your own accord, cheerfully, amicably." It's entirely the province of the *gerootn kint,* the clever, successful child that *you* can never be.

NONE TOO BRIGHT, PART II

A narrow-minded person

> HOT A KOP VEE A SHPILkeh-KEPL DEE GRAIS
> *has a head the size of a pinhead.*

A stupid person who considers herself smart

> KLERT TSEE A FLOY HOT A PIpik
> *wonders if a flea has a belly-button.*

And what you say to her is:

> STHRENG-ZHE DAIM MOYekh NISHT OON
> *Don't strain your brain.*

> VEN EER MOYekh VOLT geVAIN deenaMEET, VOLT ZEE ZAKH
> NISHT geKENT OYSshneitsn
> *If brains were dynamite, she couldn't blow her nose.*

> ER HOT A TEMPN MOYekh
> *He's dull-minded.*

> KIK IM OON, DAIM MOYfes-a-DOR
> *Look at him, the wonder of his generation.*

> ER HOT NISHT IN KOP VOOS IKH HOB IN MINDSTN NAIgeleh
> *He doesn't have* [as much] *in his head as I have in my tiniest nail.*

> ER NEMT A MEser IN GAYT ZAKH HENgen
> *He takes a knife and tries to hang himself.*

4. Epes

The Certs of the Yiddish lexicon, *Epes is* pronoun and adverb rolled into one. It means "something" or "somewhat," "something of a," and tends to cast a certain shadow of uncertainty over whatever it's been brought in to modify.

VILST Epes ESN?
Would you like something to eat?

DOOS VIL IKH NISHT. IKH VIL Epes ANdersh.
This isn't what I want. I want something else.

ER IZ Epes AN akTYOR
He's some kind of actor (there's a slight pejorative feel here,
leaving the subject just this side of "self-styled").

MEER IZ Epes HAYS
I'm kind of hot.

YOU: VEN KIMstee OON?
When you coming?

THEM: Epes AKHT A ZAYger
Sometime around eight [i.e., *anytime between six and ten*].

Epes is essential to the lack of specificity that lets praise sound like blame and makes sure that no one is ever on time:

DER SHPEEL IZ geVAIN Epes GIT
The play was good, in spite of all reasonable expectations.

6

Madness, Fury, and Driving

A clever Yiddish translation of Tolstoy's *Anna Karenina*, one striving to be more than serviceable, would open with the observation that, while every happy family is the same,

YAIDEH IMGLIKLIKHEH MISHPOOKHEH HOT EEREH AYGENEH MESHIGASN
Every unhappy family has its own causes of unhappiness,

its own *meshigasn*, "peculiarities, madnesses, whims, caprices"—what we'd now call "issues." As the nominal form of MESHIGEH, "crazy," *meshigas* has its work cut out for it. It means "madness, craze, frenzy":

VOOS FAR A MESHIGAS IZ DOOS?
What sort of madness is this?

IKH GAY KEIN MOOL NISHT EINKOYFN BAISN KRISMEHS-MESHIGAS
I never go shopping during the Christmas *insanity.*

VOOS FAR AN OYSFARKOYF HOBM MEER ITST? MITN-ZIMER MESHIGAS!
What kind of sale are we having now? Midsummer madness!

BEI BAYDEH PREZIDENTN IZ SADDAM HUSSEIN GEVORN EPES A MESHIGAS
Saddam Hussein was a sort of idée fixe *for both presidents.*

RABOYSEI, MEER GLAYBT ZAKH NISHT—DER TSHEMP IZ AREINGEFALN
IN MESHIGAS!
Ladies and gentlemen, I don't believe it—the Champ has gone berserk!

One of the Three Stooges' best-known routines revolves around the Maharajah of Meshigas, as played by Curly, while another well-known bit has Moe calling for his instruments while pretending to perform surgery: "Annamanapaneh," he starts with a nonsense term. "Annamanapaneh," echoes Larry. *"Meshigas." "Meshigas."*

Someone who suffers from a *meshigas* is, of course, *meshigeh,* an adjective that works very much like the English "crazy" or "nuts" and means everything from actually insane to extremely fond of or devoted to a person, place or thing. As Louis Prima and Keely Smith used to sing in the dialect that we're not using here, "I'm *meshuga* for my sugar/And my sugar's *meshuga* for me."

Craziness occupies an important place in Yiddish speech. While *meshigeh* is the best-known term for mental disturbance, it has plenty of competition:

BIST meTIref geVORN IN GANTSN?

Have you gone totally off your nut?

Weinreich aptly defines *metiref* as "frantic, rabid, deranged."

MAleh VOOS ER ZUGT; ER IZ A tseDRAIter

Who cares what he says? He's nuts.

The adjective *tsedrait* means "distorted, deranged; unhinged," and is quite popular in Yiddish and Yiddish-influenced English. The classic be-bop vocal, "Twisted," which opens with, "My analyst told me/That I was right out of my head," would have been called *Tsedrait* in Yiddish, because the protagonist is completely

KHOOser DAYeh

out of her mind.

Literally, though, *khooser dayeh* means "lacking in understanding," because

SEH FELT EER A KLEPkeh IN KOP

She's missing a barrel stave in her head,

i.e., she's got a screw loose, she's a few bricks shy of a load. You can get a bit closer to the English while remaining authentically Yiddish by saying

SEH FELT IM A

MIᴛᴇʀᴋᴇʜ IN KOP

He's missing a nut (as

distinct from a bolt) *in his head*

SEH FELT EER

A SHREIFL IN KOP

She's missing

a screw in her head.

If you're trying to be a little more delicate—especially if you're discussing real mental illness rather than behavior or opinions that are different from yours—you say

ER/ZEE IZ NISHT BEI ZAKH

He/She is out of their senses; not in full possession of their faculties.

ZEE IZ ᴀROOP FIN ZIɴᴇɴ

She's lost her mind.

ER IZ NISHT KEN HEEɢᴇʀ

He's not really here; he is distraught or quite upset; he is a space cadet.

Dealing with such people is going to make you as crazy as they are:

ZAY MAKHN MIKH ᴍᴇSHIɢᴇʜ

They're driving me crazy.

That's All I Can Stand

Dealing with ᴍᴇSHIGOɪᴍ day in and day out tends to keep the average Yiddish-speaker in that near-constant state of chagrined distraction characterized by the adjective ᴛsᴇ*TIMLT*. A little more merciful than *tsedrait,* a bit more forgiving, *tsetimlt* can sometimes be joined with it, as in Rodgers and Hart's

ᴛsᴇDRAIT, ᴛsᴇSHTROODLT IN ᴛsᴇTIMLT

loosely, *Bewitched, bothered and bewildered.*

Where a *tsedraiter* seems to have become unhinged just to spite the rest of the world, someone who's *tsetimlt* is confused, bewildered, unable to grasp what's going on around them:

LOZ ZEE TSE REE; ZAIST NISHT AZ ZEE IZ EPES TSETIMLT?

Leave her alone; can't you see that she's not all there [i.e., immediate circumstances—sudden tragedy or misfortune—have so discomfited her that she can scarcely be said to be in full possession of her faculties; *or*, her brain is pumping away so hard that it's about to overheat—if you work it any harder, I'm afraid that it's going to blow]?

Someone who's *tsetimlt* can also be described as

TSEKHISHT

distraught, distracted; absent-minded.

The *khish* in *tsekhisht* is the Hebrew *khish* (*khoosh* in Israeli Hebrew) which means "sense, feeling":

DER MENTSH HOT FINEf KHIshim   ER HOT A KHISH FAR DRIK-FELER

A human being has five senses   *He's got an eye for typos.*

A person who is *tsekhisht*—*tse* here means "un"—has been un-sensed, desensitized by virtue of having no grasp of what's taking place in the immediate vicinity. Numb, in other words, insensible. They're

TSESHROYFT

unscrewed, upset.

A *shroyf* is a screw, and as those great Canadians, The Guess Who, used to say, a *tseshroyfter* (or *tseshroyfteh*), has "come undone," become completely

TSESHTROODLT

confused, disturbed.

Fond as Yiddish is of baked goods and metaphors based on food and digestion, the *shtroodl* here has nothing to with the pastry that shares its name; this *shtroodl* is a whirlpool, and the *tseshtroodlter's* head is spinning in a way that Tommy Roe captured perfectly in his mid-'60s hit, "Dizzy": "I'm so dizzy, my head is spinnin'/Like a whirlpool, it never ends/And it's you, girl, makin' it spin."

All three of these adjectives also exist as regular verbs that you can use whenever you like:

TSE KHISHN   TSE SHROYFN   TSE SHTROODLN.

You can accuse others of doing these things to you and even demand that they stop: the confusion and disturbance that they're wreaking are causing you to

BLON DZHN AFN OY LEM-A-TOY EH

to wander about in limbo,

in the world of souls awaiting correction before being admitted to heaven. It's the equivalent of not knowing what world you're in in English.

Such distraction can lead quickly to frustration, a state in which

MEH KRIKHT AF DEE GLEI KHEH VENT

you're climbing the walls, the smooth, straight walls,

an idiom with the same range in Yiddish as it has in English.

MEH GAYT A RIM OON A KOP   MEH KRITST MIT DEE TSAYN

You run around in great distress   *You gnash your teeth*

[lit., "without a head"]

IN REIST ZAKH DEE HOO ER

and tear your hair

until you finally can't stand it anymore and wham!

MEH SHPRINGT FIN HOYT

you jump out of your skin [i.e., *lose your temper*]

we'd rather climb into something with wheels and heat that can serve as weapon and refuge simultaneously. And now that air-conditioning means that no car window need ever be opened again, we've embarked on a new golden age of in-car Yiddish artistry. "Why do the nations rage?" ask the Psalms (Ps. 2:1); what's with the chases, the guns, the fisticuffs? Let them take a lesson from us— we've been taking out millennia of frustration behind the wheel for decades now, with no harm to anyone but ourselves. The car has done more than any other invention to insulate us from the pains of *gooles*, of exile. Behind that wheel, every Jew is a tough guy, a SHTARker, a street-fighting man who takes crap from nobody and knows that in a car, as in space, no one can hear him scream. The air of many a Yiddish-speaker's car is heavy with slurs, slights, and threats of violence. A combative spirit takes possession of such a driver as soon as his *tukhes* touches the seat and his foot reaches the pedals; it departs just as quickly when he turns off the ignition and opens the door. King of the road becomes lord of antacids again.

Simple Insults

Simple means simple: one- or two-word verbal slaps, delivered sometimes as a single salvo, sometimes as part of a cluster-curse. Those confined to specific situations or best used in particular circumstances will be indicated as such. They're organized in loosely thematic fashion, with necessary notes at the end of each section. Additional senses of a word that might help to enhance appreciation have been given as required.

COMMON WORDS THAT MEAN "FOOL, BLOCKHEAD, PERSON OF LIMITED INTELLIGENCE" AND ARE LIKELY TO BE USED IN DAY-TO-DAY SPEECH

NAR	SHOYteh	TIpesh
fool	*fool*	*stupid person*

SHOYTEH GOOMER	SHOYTEH ben PIKHOLTS
complete/perfect fool	*fool with a woodpecker for a father*

IDYOT	GOYLEM	GOYLEM AF RAIDER
idiot	*golem*	*golem on wheels*

GOYLEM MIT A STEERING WHEEL	GOYLEM MIT A KEREVER
(more common than the next entry)	*golem with a steering wheel*

YOLD	YUKL	SHMENDRIK
dope, sap	*simpleton*	*clueless person*

KOONEH-LAIML	KHISHIM	BOTS
feckless fool	*idiot*	*dolt*

LAIKISH	BOOLVAN
simpleton	*moron, blockhead*

Nar and *shoyteh* are probably the most common ways of saying "fool," with *tipesh* a close third. A golem, of course, is the legendary clay automaton animated by the use of divine names; *goylem af raider* is an old expression that takes on new meaning when applied to a driver of unusual cluelessness, the sort who only understands how to step on the gas and go, not how to do so in the midst of other vehicles. The driving *goylem* is quite literally *af raider*; the steering wheel idioms seem to have come along after *goylem af raider* began to seem a little too obvious when talking about someone in a car.

Yold (often pronounced *yolt* when it's meant to be emphatic), which now means primarily "sap, sucker, dupe" and once in a while, "yokel, rube, hick," comes from the Hebrew and originally meant "well-born boy, scion of a wealthy family," whence it developed into "fop, popinjay." Think of a Jewish Sir Andrew Aguecheek from *Twelfth Night*—wealthy, stupid, credulous and self-absorbed—and you'll see how *yold* developed into what it is today. The yokel aspect developed out of the supposed credulousness of hicks in the hinterland, so that the word often has a sense of "mark, victim of a confidence scheme."

The *shmendrik* and the *kuneh-laiml* both entered the language through the work of Abraham Goldfadn, the self-titled "Father of the Yiddish Theater," who, in good Yiddish fashion, really *was* the father of the Yiddish theater, a fact that didn't save him from dying in poverty. *Shmendrik* and *kuneh-laiml* were originally the names of characters who embody the qualities that have come to be associated with these terms. A *shmendrik* walks (or drives) into a wall because he expects it to get out of his way; a *kuneh-laiml* didn't notice the wall to begin with. A *shmendrik* is the sort of person who made FEMA so effective both before and after Hurricane Katrina; a *yold* believes the *shmendrik*'s claim that it wasn't his fault, while the *kuneh-laiml* wants to know when the hurricane's going to hit.

Khishim (or *khushim* in some dialects)—which leans more to "idiot" than to a simple "fool," comes from the biblical Hushim, whom Genesis 46:23 describes as "the *sons* of Dan," even though there was only one of him; he was apparently so out of it that he didn't know if he was singular or plural. The Talmud (Sotah 13) portrays him as a mute who doesn't know what's going on around him. Biblical and rabbinic law once looked upon muteness as a form of feeblemindedness. Not one Yiddish-speaker in a hundred knows the origin of the term anymore, while advances in scientific understanding have brought about a change in halakhic attitudes to the deaf and the mute.

Boolvan, another great favorite, starts out meaning "tailor's dummy" and never really loses the sense that the idiot described is also clumsy or ungainly.

WORDS RARELY HEARD ANYMORE OUTSIDE
OF MOVING CARS

Fool, simpleton

YONTS	SHMOYGER	SHMEGDEH
fool, simpleton	*fool, simpleton*	*fool, simpleton*

SHMEGDEH MIT AISIK	MEKELEH	SHMOYSH
shmegdeh *with vinegar*	*fool, simpleton*	*fool, simpleton*

PEPKEH	POODELEH	POODZHELEH
fool, simpleton	*scarecrow*	*scarecrow*

The vinegar in *shmegdeh mit aisik* is one of the great intensifiers in Yiddish. It works the same way as "with bells on" or "with a cherry on top" do in English. So we get SHLIMAZL *mit aisik*, bad luck with vinegar; bad luck so complete that, like anything else preserved in vinegar, it won't be going anywhere anytime soon. So you could say that Brad Pitt *hot seks apil* [those last two words are English] *mit aisik*. You can also describe someone as being OYSGEPITST *in aisik in in* HOONIK, decked out in vinegar and honey, that is, dressed to the nines, dressed to kill, looking as hot as a herring.

Blockhead

YOLEP	STOOPEH	GETSH	PENTYUKH
oaf	*mortar*	*idol*	*blockhead*

SIMPLE INCOMPETENCE

Dawdler, ditherer, bungler (these are particularly useful when dealing with drivers who won't commit to a definite lane, who sit stubbornly still after the light has turned green, or signal for one direction and then turn in the other):

meGEgeh	shmeGEgeh	LAPN-MITSL
dawdler, ditherer, bungler	*dawdler, ditherer, bungler*	*hat with earflaps*

Shmegegeh, a contemptuous form of the now rare *megegeh* (which might not have sounded contemptuous enough for a nation of connoisseurs) is probably more prominent in Jewish English than it ever was in Yiddish. Whatever it is, the *shmegegeh* does it wrong but thinks that he's a champ; the essence of his *shmegege-hood* is his failure to realize the truth about himself and his lack of ability. He consults a manual before ever licking a stamp— which he then sticks in the wrong corner of the envelope. He isn't incompetent; he's *proudly* incompetent.

A *lapn-mitsl,* the sort of fur hat with flaps that's recently become popular again, is also a milksop, a less dangerous, more ineffectual *shmegegeh* who considers himself ready for anything. With his dripping nose projecting from the hat's earflaps like a putz from a set of bollocks, the *lapnmitsl,* or milksop, is a *shmuk* to be pitied—unless he's driving the car in front of you.

IRONIC ATTRIBUTION OF INTELLIGENCE

KHOOkhem	DREIver GOOen
Sage	*Genius of driving*

KHOOkhem-beLEIleh

Sage at night; smart when nobody's looking

Dreiver gooen seems to be used in only one form, as part of a command issued to passengers in the speaker's car:

NU, KIKTS IM OON, DAIM DREIver GOOen

Nu, look at him, [he's] the genius of driving.

Dreiver gooen—driver gaon, as it would look in a Jewish studies textbook—is a play on such titles as the Vilna Gaon, known as *der vilner gooen* in Yiddish. The Vilna Gaon (1720–1797)—the most significant Jewish scholar of the last five hundred years and hasidism's original opponent—is far from the only scholar to have had the title linked to the city or town in which he lived. Other well-known *geonim* include the Rogatchover and the Steipler, both important figures in twentieth-century orthodoxy; the latter died in 1985. To talk about a *dreiver gooen* is to suggest someone whose skill behind the wheel is a source of wonder and admiration to Jews all over the world.

RUSTICITY

POYer	ZHLOB
peasant	*peasant, boor*
KHLOP	KHAM/khaMOOleh
boor, peasant; big youth	*boor, churl, vicious peasant*

It isn't only similarity of sound that has led to the colloquial use of *zhlob* as a counterpart to the English "slob." Slovenliness and life in the sticks are associated in many cultures—think of Li'l Abner or Jed Clampett. And just imagine a culture that could have spawned a chain of family restaurants called Bob's Big *Khlop*, specializing in the double *tshoolnt* burger, had it only had the chance.

BOTANICAL ORIGINS

Best used with drivers who are slow off the mark or aren't keeping up with traffic in spite of the honking of those stuck behind them. Except for the first entry below, which means "piece of wood," all words in this section not otherwise defined have a primary meaning of "post" or "pole." They all have a secondary meaning of fool, except for *klots*, which has more to do with ungainliness and incompetence than with actual lack of capacity.

SHTIK HOLTS	DRONG	STOYP
STOLB	FLOKN	SLOOP

KLOTS	PROPN
beam	*cork*

KATSHN	GLOMP
cabbage stalk or stem	*cabbage stalk or stem*

Note that Yiddish has at least *two* words for cabbage stem.

SIGHTEDNESS

A KLOTS MIT OYGN	A SHTIK FLAYSH MIT OYGN
A wooden beam with eyes	*A piece of meat with eyes*

A SHTIK FLAYSH MIT TSVAY OYGN

A piece of meat with two eyes

HEARING

A POTS MIT OYren

a putz [or *a prick*] *with ears*

IMPLIED COMPARISON WITH ANIMALS

FERD	OKS	beHAImeh	KHAmer	AYZL
horse	*ox*	*beast, cow*	*donkey*	*donkey*

Khamer comes from Hebrew; *ayzl* is the Germanic for the same thing. Put the two together and you get *khamer-ayzl*, "skirt chaser."

beHAImeh beTSIres MENTSH	beHAImeh beTSIres DREIver
animal in human form	*animal in driver form*

KELberneh TSEEreh	TSIG	KEE
calf-face (wide-eyed incomprehension)	*goat*	*cow*

KEE MIT EIter	VANTS	PArekh
cow with an udder (of a large woman only)	*bedbug*	*mange, S.O.B.*

CRANIOLOGY

The noun *kop,* which usually means "head," is best understood as equivalent to the English "brain" in these words.

FERDSkop	KHAmerkop
horse brain	*donkey brain*

AYZLkop	GOYisher kop
donkey brain	*gentile brain*

DISEASE AND PHYSICAL INFIRMITY

MAkeh	kholYAIreh
plague, wound, blow, abscess	*cholera, nogoodnik*

PRISHtshik	TSHIrik
pimple	*pustule*

MAtseh-POOnim

matzoh face; pockmarked; acne-scarred

LOOmer	HOYker
lame, halt	*hunchback*

KALyekeh	VISteh KALyekeh
cripple	*wretched cripple*

SHLAK

stroke, nuisance, evil

A SHLAK MIN-A-sHuMEIyim

An evil nuisance visited upon us from heaven

A SHLAK FIN ZEIN LEEBM NOOmen

An evil nuisance visited upon us by Him Whose Name is to be blessed

MEEyeskeit

ugliness, ugly person; human embodiment of ugliness

Despite, or perhaps because of the number of Yiddish-speakers who use walkers, canes, and wheelchairs, Yiddish has remained stubbornly resistant to efforts to empower the disabled. My father, who had only one leg, saw no irony in screaming *kalyekeh* or *loomer* at cars with disabled stickers on their windows, or with using the same words, along with *hoyker* (which usually applied to someone hunched over the steering wheel), as insults pure and simple, without regard to the real physical condition of the person being insulted. Indeed, they were used more often for people straddling lanes, trying to parallel park, or driving too slowly (for whom the proper Yiddish term is *anybody-in-front;* those with the chutzpah to pass from behind were generally dismissed with *Gay, yug zakh; der feld 'et bald* AntLOYFN, "Come on, go as fast as you can; the cemetery's gonna run away in a minute") than for those who were living with a disability. Despite the fact that he needed two canes and a prosthesis to get to the car and could drive only with the help of hand controls, the old man saw no irony in attributing fantasy versions of his own condition to his fellow drivers. In typically Yiddish fashion, he transferred his own *tsooris*—his own troubles—to others, where they could be viewed with the scorn that they really deserved.

Matseh-poonim is the kosher-for-Passover follow-up to being a pizza face: matzohs are geSHTIPLT, perforated, with little toothed wheels called MATSEH-RAIDELAKH, matzoh wheels, which leave the finished product with a bumpy, uneven surface reminiscent of acne scars.

TOO OLD TO CUT THE MUSTARD

ALTER TAIREKH	ALTER KAKER
old fool	*old fart*

The *kaker*, as we've already seen, *drayt zakh vee a foorts in roosl*, is as purposeful as a fart in soup. The *alter tairekh* appears to have got his name from Terah, Abraham's father, who made his living as an idol dealer. Any kid with a traditional Jewish education knows that the night after Terah tells the boy Abraham that the idols are omnipotent gods, Abe sneaks into the showroom and chops them all down. When a furious Terah asks him about it the next morning, Abraham simply replies that since they're so omnipotent, they must have chopped themselves down. But Terah fails to draw the obvious conclusion and remains an idol-worshipper until the end of his days. Hence the folk-etymology here; scholars believe that the term *tairekh*—which appears nowhere else in the language—results from the assimilation of the name of Abraham's father, a well-known idiot, to a similar-sounding Slavic word that means "light-minded" or "frivolous." An *alter tairekh* is the kind of old man who comes to mind in such English proverbs as "There's no fool like an old fool." He isn't just a regular jerk; he's a natural jerk who loves to practice and has been doing so for decades.

BAD CHARACTER

GANEF	GAZLEN	KHAZER
thief	*bandit*	*pig*

DUver-Akher	HItsel/HINTshlaiger	grobYAN
"other thing,"	*dogcatcher, bum,*	*mannerless*
pig, swine	*good for nothing*	*asshole*
paskoodNYAK	meNIVL	parSHIvets
S.O.B.	*vile, despicable person*	*scurvy fellow*
OYSvurf	MAMzer	LOOMP
outcast, bum, pariah	*bastard*	*scoundrel*

We begin with the strictly metaphorical. The thief and bandit have done something to anger you, but it probably has nothing to do with theft or banditry. The difference between a *khazer* and a *duver-akher* in driving terms is that the *khazer* is a regular road-hog, the *duver-akher* forces you off the road and flips you off while doing so.

Hitsel and *hintshlaiger*, which both mean "dogcatcher," are among the most offensive words in a language not usually well-disposed to dogs. Dogs and Jews enjoyed a symbiotic relationship in the old country; the dogs were the predators and the Jews their prey. Although Yiddish is far from canine-positive, the dogcatcher gets such bad press because he was also the dog killer, and is generally portrayed as someone who loves his work. Where a *shoykhet*, a ritual slaughterer, is thought of as a pious person who is engaged in the performance of important *mitsves*, the *hitsel* likes to kill—and there's a sense that if he can't find a dog, you'll do just as well. There's an old saying that goes:

ER HOT DIKH geSHLUGN?

He hit you?

RIF IM HItsel/RIF IM HINTshlaiger

Call him hitsel/hintshlaiger.

This is a perfect example of a two-pronged insult whose second prong might not prick the victim until the speaker is safely out of reach. By the time he realizes that you've insulted *him* by calling his assailant a dog beater, it's too late for him to get hold of you. For Yiddish-speakers, who come from a religious tradition in which the name of a thing tends to be considered the same as the thing itself, it's enough to threaten violence; the Talmud tells us that he who so much as raises his hand is already considered an evildoer. Only a lunatic—a morally depraved lunatic—would ever go so far as to land an actual blow. There are no exceptions to this rule, unless you're raising children or teaching them, so the dogcatcher's willing embrace of an occupation devoted to physical cruelty was generally seen as the outward sign of a deeply rooted lack of conscience.

When it comes to oral violence, *grobyan* and *paskoodnyak* both pack a real punch; they're not the sort of the thing you want to say in front of the people you're describing unless you're willing to step outside and settle things like a couple of dogcatchers with foreskins.

Menivl is also quite useful. If Daffy Duck were to say "You're despicable" in Yiddish, he'd say, *"Dee bist a menivl."* *Parshivets* is also quite effective, and not nearly as dated as my hyperliteral translation might make it sound. Ditto for *loomp.* The *oysvurf* has been shut of the community of good drivers on account of offenses too numerous to mention.

MALE MEMBER

SHMOK	POTS	ZOONEV	VAYDL	SHVANTS

The last three all have a "clean" meaning of "animal's tail." The first two simply are what they are—in English they're usually *shmuk* and *putz*—and what they are is quite obscene; they're much stronger in Yiddish than the casual nature of their use in English might lead you to expect. *Shvants,* the equivalent of "cock" or "prick," has further extended senses that correspond to "asshole, dick, jerk"; offensive as *shvants* might be, it actually serves as the somewhat less obscene version of *pots,* and is the sort of thing that you'd say about someone who cuts you off deliberately. The *shmok* who does the same thing because he couldn't be bothered to look in his mirror is a *vaydl*—a dipshit, a moron, a fuckface, and a butthead—while *zoonev,* considerably rarer in speech than either of the other two, can be used for either type. Just think *asshole* with a capital *A,* with a heavy admixture of *shit-for-brains.*

WOMEN ONLY

TIPsheh	neKAYveh	ZAIresh
fool	*female*	*bitter and wicked woman*

KLIpeh	marSHOOes	pasKOODnitseh
shrew	*malicious/wicked woman*	*female S.O.B.*

neVAIleh
carcass; morally foul woman

aREEreh	makheSHAIfeh	KLAFteh
shrew	*witch*	*bitch*

Insulting terms about women make up in offensiveness what they lack in quantity. *Tipsheh* is the least offensive of the terms above, *klafteh* the most. While it means "human bitch"—a dog would be called a *tsoyg* or *tseigl*—*klafteh* is closer in feel to the English "cunt," and is just as likely to be forgotten or forgiven by its victim. If you use it within range of her hearing, don't be surprised if you get slapped. Even while driving, it's best to reserve it for collisions that could have been easily avoided and in which you or someone in your car has suffered fairly serious physical injury. *Klafteh* is so offensive, it's one of the very few Yiddish words that can never be used ironically.

Zairesh, known as Zeresh in English, is the wife of Haman in the biblical story of Esther. Imagine Lady Macbeth crossed with Hitler; when she isn't screaming, her lips are pursed in conspiratorial anger. She's a walking definition of fARBISN, "belligerently unyielding," and could, in the case of the original, be described as *a* fARBISeneh anti-seMITkeh, "a dyed-in-the-wool female anti-Semite." The original Zeresh is among the few people—Ilse Koch is another—whom you could describe as a *klafteh* in polite Yiddish company without embarrassing yourself and everyone around you.

A *klipeh,* literally a "husk," is an evil spirit; the term is also applied metaphorically to a particularly troublesome child. *Areereh* (*arooreh* in some dialects) means "accursed one"—cursed with having to be who she is. Worse than the *areereh,* the *marshooes* is the kind of woman who would take being called *zairesh* as a compliment. If she's committing adultery on the side, she's a *nevaileh.* *Makheshaifeh* covers the same ground as the English "witch," while the crowning insult—*nekayveh,* "female"—used only by men, encapsulates a worldview in which women have been excluded from so much that nonwomen begin to assume that incompetence must have something to do with it. It's symptomatic that the Hebrew *nekaivah* means literally "thing with a hole punched in it."

Simple Actions

Now that the enemy has been identified and labeled, what is to be done about him? Remember, we're driving. At thirty mph we're covering forty-four feet per second; this is no time for elaborate curses that build and build. You need something that can do its job before the next *yold* comes along. You also need instructions so that others sharing the road with you can benefit from your driving expertise.

The phrases that follow are the *drop deads* and *go to hells,* the *do thises* and *do thats* that no language can do without.

DRIVING INSTRUCTIONS

VUS ZITStee IN HInerplait?

Why are you sitting there in a daze?

KHAP ZAKH OYF

Wake up

TSHIkheh ZAKH OYS

Snap out of it

NU, FOOR/FEER/GAY SHOYN

Come on, go/drive/get going already

NU, TEE-ZHE SHOYN Epes

Come on, do something already

NU, YUG ZAKH

Come on, speed it up

To someone hesitating about what to do, which way to go, and so forth:

NU SHOYN?

Make up your mind already

aHEEN TSEE aHER

one way or the other

[i.e., *make up your mind*]

BEHAVIORAL INSTRUCTIONS

Ver is the imperative singular form of the verb *vern*, "to become," and is best translated as "get":

VER

Get

GeHARget

killed

derSHTIKT

suffocated

derSHTOKHN

stabbed

derSHOSN

shot

derVORGN

choked.

There are also four common commands, all of which mean "blow up" or "explode" and have an idiomatic sense of "get bent" or "screw off":

VER tseZETST   VER tsePLATST   VER tsePIKT   VER tseSHRPINGEn

And let's not forget:

VER tseSHMAItert	VER tseKOKHT IN tseBROTN
get smashed to bits	*get boiled and roasted*

VER OOPgerisn	VER OYSgerisn
get torn apart	*get torn away (from life); suffer.*

Gay is the imperative singular of the verb *gayn*, "to go."

GAY

Go

IN DR'ERD	SHLUG ZAKH KOP IN VANT
to hell [lit., "into the ground"]	*bang your head against the wall*

KAKN AFN YAM

shit on the sea.

Although often misunderstood, *gay kakn afn yam* is among the best known and most popular of all Yiddish curses. You don't shit *in* the sea, you shit *on* it; you're supposed to balance on the surface of the water, struggling to retain your equilibrium and keep from drowning while trying to take care of a delicate business. Yiddish-speakers have long been aware that most of their neighbors believe that Jesus walked on water; *gay kakn afn yam* doesn't only refer to this famous walk, it demands that you surpass Jesus and step aside for a private moment on—and not in—the Sea of Galilee.

MORE JESUS CHRIST

GAY KAKN AFN YAM is part of a significant body of Yiddish material devoted to the mockery of Jesus and denial of Christianity. As the Crusades, the Saint Bartholomew's Day Massacre, and the pogroms of the nineteenth and twentieth centuries, to give but three examples, have taught us, religion can be a hands-on business, especially for the religion with the larger number of hands. European Jews were the handled, not the handlers, and they responded as they always do: with their mouths.

This type of response was hardly new. Since the destruction of the Temple, says Rabbi Nakhmen in a well-known Talmudic passage, "All joking is forbidden except for jokes about idol worship" (Sanhedrin 63b). In societies in which virtually every activity takes on a religious cast, such an injunction doesn't prohibit very much.

Even if we confine ourselves to expressions that are still vaguely current, we don't have to look very far for material. If you're talking about a woman weighed down with too much jewelry, especially if it's cheap and garish, you can say that

ZEE SHLEPT DAIM TOLEH AF ZAKH AROYF
She's hoisting the hanged one [i.e., Jesus] *up onto herself,*

she's wearing everything but the kitchen sink—i.e., you'll probably find a crucifix somewhere in there, too.

A crucifix is sometimes called a *yoyz* (a cross per se, as well as a crucifix, is known as a *TSAILEM*, very literally, "an image"). *Yoyz* is a shortened form of *Yoyzl*, which, like *YOSHkeh*, is a diminutive of *yeHoySHOOa*, Joshua, the full form of Jesus' Hebrew name. *Yoshkeh* is still relatively common in Yiddish as a nickname for Jewish Joshuas; when used about Jesus, it's rather like calling him "Li'l Josh." Both diminutives are used to avoid mention of Jesus' actual name. *Yoshkeh* is sometimes used on its own, sometimes coupled with *PANdreh*, as in *Yoshkeh Pandreh*, i.e., Jesus the son of Pantheras, a Roman centurion said to have been Jesus' father in some Jewish traditions. *Yoyzl* is generally coupled with *pots*—and that's all she wrote.

Yoyz itself has a number of senses beyond "crucifix."

OY, ER ZITST DORTN VEE A LAYMENER GOYLEM, VEE A YOYZ
Oy, he's sitting there like a clay golem, like a dummy.

continued...

Since the person on the crucifix doesn't talk, the image becomes identified with the gods described in the Psalm: "They have hands, but do not feel; feet, but do not walk and they do not make a sound in their throat" (Ps. 115:7)—dummies, in other words.

Frequent exposure to paintings of the Passion led to the development of the phrase *GELER YOYZ*:

ER IZ NEbakh NISHT geZINT, ER ZAIT OYS VEE A GELer YOYZ
The poor man isn't well, he's sickly and sallow [lit., "looks like a jaundiced Jesus"].

Children used *yoyz* to mean "sourpuss" when describing an adult and "crybaby" when referring to another kid. There's also the fabulous

YOYZL-YOYKH
Jesus juice [lit., "Jesus soup"],

which was soldiers' slang for lousy coffee.

THINGS THAT SHOULD COME UPON YOU

A SHVARTS-YOOR AF DEER
A plague [lit., "black year, devil"] *on you*

A VISteh PGEEreh AF DEER
A dismal animal-death on you

A farTSEEkenish AF DEER
May you be eaten alive
[lit., "a devouring upon you"]

A FINster MAZL AF DEER
May your luck be dark
[lit., "dark luck on you"]

A ZOKHN IN DEER
*May a nonspecific but utterly
debilitating illness take you over*

**A kholYAIreh ZOL
DIKH KHAPN**
May you be seized by the cholera

MORE THINGS TO DO

KISH MIKH IN TUkhes

Kiss my ass

KISH MIKH VEE DEE YEEDN HOBM geREET

Kiss me where the Jews reposed [i.e., *kiss my ass*]

IKH HOB DIKH IN BUD

To hell with you [lit., "I have you in the bath"]

The *bud* or bath often serves as a polite stand-in for hell: a deep pit in the ground with a big fire burning in it can't help but call forth images of that other fiery pit. *Ikh hob dikh in bud* has exactly the same meaning as *ikh hob dikh in dr'erd*—in both cases, as far as *I'm* concerned, *you* can go straight to hell.

A REEyekh IN DEIN	A REEyekh IN DEIN TAtens
TAten aREIN	TAten aREIN
An evil spirit in	*An evil spirit in your*
your father	*father's father*

A *reeyekh* is generally thought of as the soul of a deceased being, a ghost. Once it enters a living person, it is known as a *dybbuk*—from a Hebrew word meaning "to cleave, to cling"—and takes over the host's body and mind. I'm not sure where the *reeyekh* is supposed to enter the victim, and I'm not really sure that it matters. In the days before modern psychology, the *reeyekh* was thought to be the cause of mental illness—and mental illness was considered hereditary. If your father had it, so did you. It's an odd, often retroactive curse, that's basically come to mean "screw you"; adding "your father's father" is like saying "and the horse you rode in on."

OTHER THINGS THAT SHOULD HAPPEN TO YOU

farKHAPT ZOLstee VERN

You should die suddenly

ZOL DEER DINern IN DEE TSAYN/IN BOYekh/IN DEE HOYZN

May it thunder in your teeth/in your belly/in your pants

VAIrem ZOLN DIKH ESN

Worms should eat you

A geSHVEER DEER IN LAIber

An abscess in your liver

To someone driving too slowly:

VILST KRIKHN? ZOLST MEER KRIKHN AFN BOYekh

You wanna crawl? You should crawl on your belly.

BIST KRANK TSE FOORN? ZOL MEN DIKH FEERN

You're not able to drive [lit., *"you're too sick . . ."*]*? You should be conveyed*
[sc., *to hospital or cemetery*—this one baffled me as a kid].

To someone who dares honk at you:

FEIFST AF MIR? IKH FEIF AF DIR

You honking at me? Then the hell with you.

This is based on a play on the verb *feifn*, which means "to whistle, to pipe (as on a fife); to honk a car horn." *Der feifer feift*, "the
piper pipes," would be an accurate description of many a Fourth
of July presentation. *Feifn af* someone or something, "to whistle
on it," though, means to blow it off, to look so far down on it that
you don't even see it; it isn't worth caring about, so you'll ignore
it—while making sure that it knows that you're ignoring it. It's a
slightly more polite way of saying that you have something *in
dr'erd* or *in bud*, as we saw above:

ER HOT MIKH IN BUD	ZEE HOT MIKH IN DR'ERD
He thinks little of me	*She thinks little of me*

IKH HOB IM IN BUD	IKH HOB ZEE IN DR'ERD
To hell with him	*To hell with her.*

Finally, when you beat out at least one other car and slide gloatingly into the last parking space:

ZOL ES ZAY OYSshtekhn DEE OYGN

May it poke their eyes out (i.e., may the sight of my triumph so disturb them that they'd rather go blind than witness it).

VOLKSWAGENS, MERCEDES BENZES, ETC.

I knew that the world I grew up in was gone for good when I noticed three or four Volkswagens and a couple of BMWs in the parking lot of my daughter's Hebrew day school, all of them utterly unmolested.

When I was a kid, you couldn't park such a car at any Jewish institution and expect to come back to windows that were intact or tires that hadn't been slashed. It was bad enough that non-Jews had such short memories, but the idea that a Jew would buy *anything*, let alone something that probably needed financing, when he knew that the money was going to *them*—that was too much to bear.

Things were so bad that in the late '60s, when a friend's older brother paid fifty dollars for what had to have been a fifth-hand Bug, he was not only forbidden to park it in the family driveway, but his neighbors in Toronto's Bathurst Manor, a Jewish area with an unusually high concentration of Holocaust survivors, not only refused to let him park on their street, they made it clear that they'd trash the car if he dared to do so—and he should also forget about *ever* going *anywhere* with any of their daughters ever again.

They made this clear in Yiddish, which the *Hitler-krikher,* as they called him, understood perfectly. As I sat waiting for my daughter to come out of school, I wondered how many of those neighbors were spinning in their graves.

The terms that follow constitute the only exceptions to the closed window rule of automotive cursing. For these, the windows were rolled all the way down, heads were stuck out, and *Hitlergrüsse* freely offered by our fathers, sometimes with the end of a pocket comb held under their noses.

HITLER

NAZI

antisemIT

antisemite

HOOmen

Haman

aMOOlek

Amalek (tribe of biblical anti-Semites)

SOYneh TSEEyen

enemy of Zion

TSOYrer hayeHEEdim

enemy of the Jews

KRAUT

DEITCH

German

HOOren-FOLK

whore race

HERenPOTS

master putz

reTSAYekh

murderer

MERder

murderer

EIGHT THINGS TO SAY IN GERMANY

1. EER DEITSHN ZENT A FEIN FOLK, NOR DOOS LOOSHN HARGET EIKH aVEK.

   You Germans are a lovely people, but your language is doing you in. (Back when it was in the third person, this was a real pre–World War II Yiddish saying.)

2. milKHOOmeh? S'IZ geVAIN DOO A milKHOOmeh?

   War? What war?

3. ER IZ AN oysTRALyer, DER MEL GIBson? TSEITN derLAIBT!

   Mel Gibson's Australian? Times have sure changed!

4. geDENK-ZHE VER ES HOT farSHPEELT DAIM KREEG!

   Just remember who lost the war!

5. ES FRAIT MIKH AZ DEE KLEZmer mooZEEK IZ aZOY popooLER HEINT IN DEITSHLANT.

   I'm glad that klezmer music is so popular in Germany today.

6. YO, IKH BIN TAkeh A YEED.

   Yes, I really am a Jew.

7. NAYN, IKH HOB GOORnisht KEIN KLEZmer komPAKtelakh BEI MEER IN SHTEEB.

   No, I have no klezmer CDs in my house at all.

8. derKLER MEER NISHT *MEIneh* "kooltooRELeh hisKHEIvesn," DEE FEEloseMIT!

   Don't tell me my "cultural obligations," you philosemite!

Five Little Words That Will Get You
Through Any Yiddish Conversation

---

5. SHOYN

Shoyn is probably the single most useful and versatile word in the entire language. Its dictionary meanings of "already, at once," barely hint at the wealth of meaning and nuance that it can hold. Used either assertively or interrogatively, *shoyn* can serve as a sufficient response to just about any barrage of Yiddish words. You can have entire conversations in which people always get something out of your *shoyns* without realizing that you haven't understood a single word that they've said to you.

Were someone, for example, to tell you that they'd just finished reading *War and Peace,* you could counter with any of the following:

> *Shoyn?* (At long, long last. What took you so long?)
>
> *Shoyn!* (*Mazl tov!* Welcome to the nineteenth century.)
>
> *In* [and] *shoyn!* (Thank God. Now you need never read anything again.)

Likewise, if you've just been informed that the Messiah has arrived:

> *Shoyn!* (It's about time.)
>
> *Shoyn?* (So soon? I hadn't finished sinning.)
>
> *In shoyn!* (It's the end of the world as we know it.)

As mentioned, the basic meanings of *shoyn* are "already, at once." So you say things like

DER FREELing IZ SHOYN geKIMen

Spring has already come

IKH GAY SHOYN

I'm going at once (usually translated literally as "I'm going already")

GeNIG SHOYN
Enough already

SHOYN GeNIG OON DAIM
Enough as it is [lit., "enough already without it"].

Shoyn is also used to convey a sense of imperfection; not that things aren't good enough as they are—a sense that all of Yiddish is used to convey—but that you've been doing something for a while and are still doing it now, you've been in a particular state from which you have yet to emerge:

VEE LANG BISTee SHOYN IN aMERikeh?
How long have you been in America (already)?

VEE LANG ZENT EER SHOYN A DOKter?
How long have you been a doctor for?

While a good translation will omit the "already," properly idiomatic Yiddish demands the presence of a *shoyn* in such questions. And it isn't only questions:

IKH BIN DOO SHOYN FInef IN DREIsik YOOR
I've been here for thirty-five years (already).

Shoyn can also be used in an almost contrary sense, to show that things have changed considerably between then and now:

NEKHTN HOT ER geVOLT IN HEINT SHOYN NISHT
He wanted it yesterday but has changed his mind [lit., "but today already not"].

Shoyn nisht, the idiom seen in the sentence above, means "no more, no longer." As John Carradine says in *The Grapes of Wrath,*

IKH BIN SHOYN NISHT KA' MAgid
I ain't a preacher no more; I have ceased to be a preacher.

continued...

If you want to express disbelief in the form of a question, you can use NISHT SHOYN ZHE, as in

NISHT SHOYN ZHE IZ PEmleh ENdesen A REbetsin?
Pamela Anderson is a rabbi's wife? [i.e., *You're not trying to tell me that Pamela Anderson is married to a rabbi?*]

You can describe the end of any enterprise, especially a sudden or abrupt end, by saying

IN SHOYN
and that's all.

ER KIMT aREIN, baLAYdikt MIKH, IN SHOYN
He comes in, insults me, and that's all she wrote.

If you can't stand to listen to someone anymore, if you're offering an ultimatum or making a definitive statement of your own, you can slam your fist down and say,

IN SHOYN,

and if they can already speak Yiddish, they'll know better than to say a word. ❧

CARDS AND CHESS PIECES

The four suits of a deck of cards are

SHEL
diamonds

ROYT
hearts

GRIN
spades

AYKHL
clubs

The picture cards are

AYBER
jack

MALKEH
queen

MAILEKH
king

TOYZ
ace

See the box on page 44 for the names of number cards. A card is called a *KORT* or a *KLAF*. To shave a deck is *MALN KLO*FIM, "to circumcise the cards." This kind of cheating is called *SHAK*RES. A card-cheat is known as a *KOZVAN*YETS, which comes from *KAZVN*, a liar.

The pieces in a chess set are

PYON
pawn

RITER
knight

LAFER
bishop

TUREM
rook

MAILEKH
king

MALKEH
queen

7

Health and Illness

The Body and Its Parts

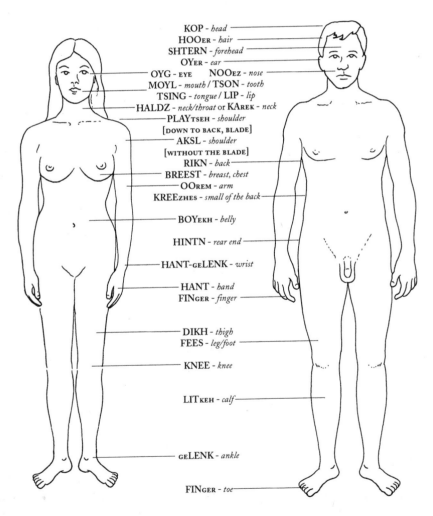

KOP - *head*
HOOer - *hair*
SHTERN - *forehead*
OYer - *ear*
OYG - eye NOOez - *nose*
MOYL - *mouth* / TSON - *tooth*
TSING - *tongue* / LIP - *lip*
HALDZ - *neck/throat* or KArek - *neck*
PLAYtseh - *shoulder*
[DOWN TO BACK, BLADE]
AKSL - *shoulder*
[WITHOUT THE BLADE]
RIKN - *back*
BREEST - *breast, chest*
OOrem - *arm*
KREEzhes - *small of the back*

BOYekh - *belly*

HINTN - *rear end*

HANT-geLENK - *wrist*

HANT - *hand*
FINger - *finger*

DIKH - *thigh*
FEES - *leg/foot*

KNEE - *knee*

LITkeh - *calf*

geLENK - *ankle*

FINger - *toe*

You can't say where it hurts if you don't know what it's called. The proper ways of indicating discomfort are:

SE TIT MEER VAY X

X hurts me,

where X = definite article + body part, in the singular;

SE TEEN MEER VAY Y

Y hurt me,

when there's more than one of the same part.

SE TIT MEER VAY DER KOP	SE TEEN MEER VAY DEE FEES
My head hurts; I've got a headache.	*My feet hurt.*

WHAT ISN'T IN THE PICTURE

Some things are just too hard to show. Among the more important of these are

NAIGL	BLIT	SHPEIEKHTS	MUSKLEN	SHEDREH
nails	*blood*	*saliva*	*muscles*	*spine.*

Most names for the reproductive organs will be found in the chapter on sex. The doctor's office names for male parts are:

PENIS	AYVER	MEELEH
penis	*member*	*circumcision.*

You don't have to use all of them. *Penis* makes it sound as if you think that you're the doctor and are briefing a colleague on the latest development in penile research. It's a little pretentious, unless you actually are a physician or similar highly trained professional who has earned the title of doctor in accordance with the recognized divisions of Yiddish-speaking academia:

A DOKter A DOKter; A DOKter A denTIST; A DOKter A filoZOF

A doctor a doctor; a doctor a dentist; a doctor a Ph.D.

Optometrists and accountants need not apply. Such professions are perfectly fine for men in search of a good living and a respectable occupation; it's just that such men are as qualified to say *penis* as they are to supervise a space launch. Like most of us, they'll have to content themselves with saying *ayver*—if they so much as try a *penis*, the doctor will be quick to put them in their place:

PATIENT: DOKter, SE TIT MEER VAY DER PEnis.
Doctor, my penis hurts.

DOCTOR: *PEnis* NOKH? *PEnis* TIBI DOLET? HERCULE! MONSTRA MIHI.
Penis yet? [Latin:] *Your penis hurts? Good God! Show it to me.*

The very tone of the word *penis* should let the pretender to learning know that he's made a mistake: he should have been saying *ayver. Ayver*, literally "member," is the standard polite term for the penis. Even though the word can be used for any of the limbs or members of the body, the presence of the definite article *der* usually makes your meaning clear. A complaint about your *ayver* won't cause the doctor to ask which one:

PATIENT: DOKter, S'IZ MEER A BREnenish IN AYver BAISN—
Doctor, there's a burning sensation in my ayver *when I—*

DOCTOR: IKH farSHTAY SHOYN. LOmeer GAIBM A KIK.
I know what you mean. Let's take a look.

Polite as it is, *ayver* can be a touch graphic for many more observant Yiddish-speakers, who tend to call it *meeleh*, "circumcision," an interesting substitution of past action for current location. It's like calling your fingertip a manicure.

The situation with testicles is the opposite of that with penis. While Uriel Weinreich's dictionary doesn't mark BAYtseh (plural,

BAY*TSIM*), the most common term, as vulgar, I don't know anybody who'd use it in front of his mother. If you've *nebakh* got to show them to your doctor, call them TES*TIKLEN*—he'll forgive you for using the technical term instead of kvetching about your balls.

Women speaking to a doctor refer to their reproductive organs simply as *dortn,* "there." Polite Yiddish is so uncomfortable with such matters that I've consigned all terms for women's genitalia to chapter 8, which deals with sex.

A BAR MITZVAH OF BEHINDS

THIRTEEN DESIGNATIONS FOR THE HUMAN REAR
(IN DECLINING ORDER OF POLITENESS)

HINTN	HIN*ter*KHAY*lek*
Rear	*Hindpart*

IN*ter*KHAY*lek*	*ge*ZES
Underpart	*Seat, buttocks*

ZITS*er*	ZITS*flaysh*
Sitter, seat	*Seat-meat*

*me*KHEEL*eh*	DER VEE-HAYST-MEN-ES
I beg your pardon	*The whatchamacallit*

VEE-DEE-YEEDN-HOBM-*ge*REET	OO*kher*
Where the Jews reposed	*Rear, behind*

*akho*REI*yim*	MORSH	TU*khes*
Hindparts	*Ass*	*Ass*

continued...

The first four are polite and self-explanatory. If you needed to talk to the doctor, you'd use *hintn* in preference to any of the others. *Gezes* isn't quite cute, but is getting awfully close, while *zitser* has definitely crossed the line:

IKH VIL NISHT AZ DER ZITSer ZOL MEER aROYSshtartsn FIN BUD-kosTYOOM
I don't want my seat to stick out of my bathing suit.

In nonanatomical usage, a *zitser* is someone who spends most of his time in a particular place; in prewar European Yiddish, a *ZITSerkeh*—that's the feminine form—was a market woman, someone who sat at her stall all day; a *bes-MEDresh zitser* did the same thing in the study-house, but without any hope of earning a living.

Zitsflaysh also has a colloquial meaning of "patience for prolonged effort, perseverance"; it has the same meaning in English, which has borrowed the term from German.

Mekheeleh and *vee-hayst-men-es* are already getting priggish, while *vee-dee-yeedn-hobm gereet*, "where the Jews rested," is a nice example of *khayder* or schoolroom wit: according to Numbers 33:26, the Israelites sojourned in a place called Tukhes—so go ahead and kiss my summer camp. *Ookher* and its plural *akhoreiyim* are simply the Hebrew for *hintn* and *hinterkheylek*. As often happens when Yiddish has doublets of this type—Hebrew and German words with identical meanings—the Hebrew becomes the vulgar (and occasionally obscene) version, probably to help facilitate cursing in public places. That's certainly what has happened here.

Tukhes is among the best-known of all Yiddish words and has been so for a long time. In his *Seyfer ha-Tishbi*, a dictionary of Talmudic and midrashic words published in 1541, Elijah Levita, who also wrote the *Boveh Beekh* mentioned on page 144, comments in his entry for *ookher*:

> The anus is called *ookher* . . . and thus: "And all their hinder
> parts [their *ookhers*] were inward" (1 Kings 7:25). And the
> common people call it [the *ookher*] *tukhes.*

It isn't vulgar; it's tradition. And so is *morsh,* which is probably related
to the Germanic *Arsch.*

INTERNAL ORGANS

BLINDEH KISHKEH *blind* kishkeh, *appendix*	**PENKHER** *bladder*	**MOYEKH** *brain*
GROBEH KISHKEH *fat* kishkeh, *colon*	**GAL** *gall bladder*	**HARTS** *heart*
GEDAIREM *intestines*	**KISHKEH** *intestine*	**NEERN** *kidneys*
LAIBER *liver*	**LINGEN** *lungs*	**VAISHET** *esophagus*
LINKEH KAIL *esophagus*	**INTERMUGN-DREEZ** *pancreas*	**SHLEIM-DREEZ** *pituitary gland*
PROSTAT *prostate*	**HOYT** *skin*	**MILTS** *spleen*
MUGN *stomach*	**SHILD-DREEZ** *thyroid gland*	**MANDLEN** *tonsils*

OODER *vein*	**TRAKHT** *womb*

The appendix and colon really are referred to as the blind and fat kishkas, respectively. In attempting to describe a colonoscopy to an aged relative with whom I have no common language but Yiddish, I could think of nothing else to say but:

MEH SHTIPT A foTO-apaRAT IN PEE-taBA'as aREIN
They shove a camera into your anus,

RIKT IM MIT A RAIreleh DORKH DER karKASHteh aDOrekh,
slide it through your rectum by means of a tube,

BIZ MEH KIKT IN GROber KISHkeh aREIN
until they're looking into your fat kishka [i.e., the colon],

to which his only response was:

MEH DARF baTSOOLN?
Do you have to pay?

And speaking of kishka, the rectum, referred to above as *karkashteh*, is sometimes—far less often, in my experience—called a *GROdeh KISHkeh*, a "straight kishka," while the duodenum, home of the ulcers that constituted the real passage to manhood for the generation before my own, is known in Yiddish as *der TSVELF-FINger kishkeh*, the twelve-fingered kishka that appears on the menu of no delicatessen on earth. *Tsvelf-finger* is, regrettably, just a translation of the Latin *duodeni*, "twelve to each," a description of the duodenum's supposed twelve-finger breadth.

If you're alive,

ES KLAPT DOOS HARTS
Your heart beats,

and any doctor will be happy to take your

PULS   *or*   DAIfek

pulse.

Some Other Things to Do with Your Body
Some common physical processes and activities:

SHNEIDN ZAKH TSAYner	KVETSHN MIT DEE PLAYtses
to teethe, cut teeth	*to shrug your shoulders*

SHVITSN	SHVITSN VEE A BEEber	SHLUFN
to sweat	*to sweat profusely* [lit., "like a beaver"]	*to sleep*

TSEEmakhn MIT AN OYG

to fall asleep, grab some shut-eye [lit., "to close an eye"]

KHAPN A DRIML

to take [lit., "grab"] *a nap.*

Dreaming in Yiddish isn't quite the same as dreaming in English. Aside from the language difference, *you* don't actually do the dreaming in Yiddish; rather, whatever you're dreaming about dreams itself *for* you (and for you alone). The verb is *KHOOlemen* and you say

MEER KHOOlemt ZAKH

or

ES KHOOlemt ZAKH MEER

I'm dreaming [lit., "it dreams itself to/for me"].

ES HOT ZAKH MEER geKHOOlemt

I had a dream.

Just think of Irving Berlin and you'll never go wrong:

ES KHOOlemt ZAKH MEER A VEIser NITL

I'm dreaming of a white Christmas.

A nightmare is

A BAYzer KHOOlem

or

A koshMAR.

Only the *bayzer khoolem* comes up in curses, generally in the plural and with an "all" thrown in for bad luck:

Aleh BAYzeh khaLOYmes TSE ZEIN KOP
May all (my) evil dreams be on his head.

Health

It's nothing to boast about in any language, especially not in Yiddish. Voluble as it often is about what can go *wrong* with you, Yiddish is uncharacteristically tight-lipped when it comes to what's right. Assuming that anything's okay, why risk screwing it up by exposure to evil spirits and jealous listeners?

Health is called geZINT; we've already seen *zei gezint* as the usual way of bidding someone farewell, along with such versions of *bon voyage* as *gay gezint* and *foor gezinterhayt*. Someone who is generally *gezint* is said to be *mit Alemen*, "with everything, a hundred percent":

MEER farBRENgen ZAKH ZAYer GIT DOO IN ZEnen Aleh MIT Alemen
We're having a wonderful time here and everybody is healthy.

If you're not well you're

NISHT MIT Alemen
not with everything.

In many dialects, though, saying that

MENDL IZ NISHT MIT Alemen
Mendel is not with everything,

is taken to mean that Mendel is not all there; he's sick, all right, but only in the head.

You can move from the head to the heart and say with the late James Brown,

MEER IZ GIT AFN HARTSN

I feel good.

And if that isn't the case?

MEER IZ SHLEKHT AFN HARTSN

I feel bad.

These are slightly expanded versions of

MEER IZ GIT   MEER IZ SHLEKHT

I'm okay, I'm doing all right   *I'm not so okay, I'm not doing*
too well.

Illness

The standard adjective for sick is

KRANK,

though by my family at home *krank* was considered too, uh, *direct,* so we used to say

SHLAF

instead. While both words have the same idiomatic meaning, the primary meaning of *shlaf* is "weak, feeble," i.e., "not with every-thing." It's thus considered a little less in-your-face than *krank,* ironically so in light of the fact that *krank* itself was originally a euphemism for *siech* (compare the English *sick*), which survives in contemporary Yiddish only as *zokhn,* a pejorative term meaning "to be sick" that is hardly heard outside of curses anymore. Like *shlaf, krank* originally meant weak, a meaning preserved to a degree in the verb *krenkn*, as we saw in such yell-classics as

KRENKST OYFtseEFenen DEE TEER?

which we can now understand aright as

Do you lack the strength/are you too weak to open the door?

rather than "are you too sick."

Someone who is sick

IZ NISHT IN GANTSN

is not in a state of wholeness,

not, as we saw above, with everything. Someone who is very sick is said to be

KHOrev

[lit., "destroyed, laid waste"].

Farbei, which means "past, by, over," figures in the idiom

ZEIN farBEI

to be on the verge of death, to be in a hopeless situation

IKH BIN farBEI

It's all over, there's no hope for me.

Farbei can also be joined to *khorev* to produce the far from uncommon *khorev farbei,* which combines the worst of both worlds.

A person that ill can be uncharitably described in animal terms:

ER ZAIT OYS VEE A gePAYgerteh KATS

He looks like a dead cat.

COVER YOUR MOUTH

Coughs, sneezes, hiccups, yawns, and burps are among the preferred crises of health in Yiddish. They are rarely serious and always give somebody a chance to say, "I told you so." Virtually the first precept of Yiddish domestic life is a negative one:

KENST ZAKH khoLIleh farKEELN

You could catch, God forbid, a cold,

in which *khoLIleh,* the "God forbid," stands in for the English "your death of." No one ever simply *farKEELT zakh,* catches cold, in Yiddish; if there's no "God forbid," the virus is dead.

The Yiddish for a cold is

KAter,

which is similar to the English "catarrh." Prophylaxis is possible in a number of ways, depending on circumstance, but there are three rules that apply at all times, in all climes:

1. Keep your collar buttoned. Don't care what you look like, care what your parents will look like if they should have to sit shiva for you:

   NU, TOM JONES, SAMMY DAVIS JR., JUNIOR, VOOS GAYStee
   ZAKH IM A tseKHRASteter?
   *Nu, Tom Jones, Sammy Davis Jr., Junior, why are you going around
   with your top buttons open?*

   DOO IZ NISHT LAS VEGAS—MEH LEKHTST ZAKH NISHT
   DEER EINtseKIKN IN PIpik
   This isn't Las Vegas; nobody's dying to get a look at your belly button.

   farKNEPL DOOS HEMD, HUGH HEFNER, KENST ZAKH
   khoLIleh farKEELN
   Button your shirt, Hugh Hefner, you could God forbid catch cold.

SHPEELN IN Eser MAkes
playing ten plagues,

because of the way in which guests at a Passover seder dip a finger in and out of their wineglass when the ten plagues visited upon the Egyptians are enumerated—a whole new way of integrating religion into daily life.

To return to the bosoms, *tsitskes*—the diminutive of *tsitses*—is far and away the most common of the slightly vulgar terms for women's breasts.

Pazookheh, on the other hand, only sounds like it should be dirty. It's probably got nothing to do with the English "bazooka" (Bob Burns, who coined the term, seems to have derived it from "bazoo," an old slang term for "mouth"); *pazookheh* (add -*es* for the plural) is a perfectly respectable Slavic word that's also perfectly respectable in Yiddish. It's the opposite of *tsitses* in that it sounds completely filthy, a fact that makes it all the more fun around moralizing types with an imperfect knowledge of the language.

DAdim	MOYsheh ve-Arendlakh	YUkheen oo-VOYez
tits	*little Moses and Aaronses*	*Jachin and Boaz*

It's a whole line of boobs from the Bible. *Dadim* is quite vulgar; although it appears in the Bible (see Ezekiel, chapter 23), it does so with reference to bad girls who let themselves be felt up. It's the sort of word that we'd see more often if there were more Yiddish porn in print: the Yiddish edition of *Juggs* would probably be called *Dadim*. Oddly enough, the singular—*dad* (rhymes with "mud")—never really crossed over from Hebrew to Yiddish.

Moysheh ve-arendlakh develops from allegorical interpretations of the Song of Songs that claim that the two breasts described in chapter 4, verse 5 ("Your two breasts are like two fawns, twins of a

gazelle, that feed among the lilies") stand for the two great nur-
turers of the Jewish people, Moses and Aaron. To say

ZEE HOT SHAYneh MOYsheh ve-Arendlakh

She's got nice little Moses and Aaronses,

is to pretend to take such an interpretation at face value. The phrase
itself comes closer to "She's got some front end on her" than to anything that you're likely to hear on a Bible-quoting TV show.

Yukheen oo-voyez is a much more straightforward reference to
the Bible. According to 1 Kings 7:21 and 2 Chronicles 3:17,
King Solomon set up two bronze pillars outside the Temple
vestibule, one of which was called *Yukheen* (Jachin in English),
the other *Voyez* (Boaz). They were about six feet thick and
twenty-seven feet tall. When a well-stacked woman walks by,
Yiddish-speaking rakes turn to each other and whistle apprecia-
tively. "*Yukheen oo-Voyez,*" they'll say; her breasts are as large and
well-formed as the pillars of the Temple, which supported only
themselves and nothing more. This bosom is giving them some
stiff competition.

BILkelakh

rolls, buns

Unlike the English *buns*, which refers to the buttocks and seems
to be crying out for a hot dog, a *BILkeleh* is a little *bilkeh*, a rounded
bun with a base that is larger than its top, and that is already complete in itself.

The Main Event
Some of the more respectable terms for intercourse are:

baHEFtung	BEIshluf
joining, copulation	*sleeping with*

BEEyeh	TASHmish-ha-MEEteh
coitus	*use of the bed, intercourse.*

The verbal equivalents of these nouns are

baHEFTN ZAKH	baSHLUFN	meSHAmesh-ha-MEEteh ZEIN
to copulate	*to sleep with*	*to use the bed, have intercourse, cohabit.*

Poor little *beeyeh*, a Talmudic favorite, has no verbal form in Yiddish; *meshamesh-ha-meeteh zein*, the preferred rabbinic and religious term, is about as close as it comes. Should you want to use this verb, remember that in the past tense you'd say,

NEKHTN BEI NAKHT HOB IKH meSHAmesh-ha-MEEteh geVAIN

Last night I cohabited.

It's the rare native-speaker who talks like this in any language. More colloquial but still respectable ways of referring to the sex act are:

SHLUFN MIT

to sleep with

or, on Yiddish-language late night Christian TV,

KHOYtenen

to sin, fornicate.

Some of the more fun-filled ways of discussing the whole business include:

TRENen	YENTSN	SHTUPN
to screw [lit., "to rip"]	*to fuck*	*to poke, fuck* [lit., "to stuff"]

SHMINTSN	YUGN ZAKH
to screw, plank	*to mate* (used of animals).

Trenen and *shtupn* are probably the most frequently used of these terms. Note the different usages for male and female subjects:

ER TRENT A SAKH VEIвеr

He screws a lot of women

ZEE TRENT MIT A SAKH MEnеr

She screws a lot of men

ZEE HOT IM TAкеh A SHTUP gеGAIBM?

Did she really give him a fuck?

ER HOT EER gеGAIBM A SHTUP?

Did he slip her a screw?

аZOY. ER HOT ZEE TAкеh gеSHTUPT

That's right. He really fucked her.

The sexual meanings of both *trenen* and *shtupn* have developed from the words' more innocent senses. The clean meaning of *trenen* is "to rip," the way a tailor rips a seam; *shtupn's* is "to stuff, fill":

ER SHTUPT DOOS MOYL

He stuffs his mouth,

is an idiomatic way of saying that someone is stuffing his face.

Yentsn comes from the neuter pronoun *yents*, "that," "the other," and was once a sexual euphemism similar to *it* in English. Frequent use eventually made it seem as filthy and forbidden as the word for which it was substituting, and it is now probably the "dirtiest" word in the language; so dirty, indeed, that it's used far more often in a nonsexual sense these days to mean "to screw, swindle, cheat," because it has become too pejorative for simple fucking.

Shmintsn is good old-fashioned, straight-ahead vulgarity. To quote Isaac Bashevis Singer,

ZEE HOT ɢᴇSHMINTST MIT A KLEZᴍᴇʀ
She was getting it on with a musician.

Yugn zakh is properly used of animals that are mating. Applied to human beings, it's similar to the English "fuck like bunnies":

ZAY YUGN ZAKH VEE ʙᴇHAYᴍᴇs
They do it like animals—

anyway, anyhow, anywhere. And all the time.

Aside from the highly technical ᴏʀɢᴀᴢᴍ, the verb ᴋɪᴍᴇɴ, "to come," seems to be the most popular North American term for reaching a climax. It might well have been influenced by English, but we shouldn't forget that German also uses the verb *kommen* in a similar sense. The great-grandparents whom I've asked about prewar European sex-Yiddish have all told me to shut up. Two or three mentioned that they had heard others—bums, of course— use slang terms borrowed from the local non-Jewish vernacular, which means that we might as well stick with *kimen* if we want to get our message across:

OY, ᴀZOY, ᴀZOY, ᴀZOY, IKH KIM SHOYN BALT
Oy, that's right, that's right, that's right, I'm gonna come any second now

OY, TAᴛᴇɴʏoo ZIsᴇʀ, VAY IZ MEER, OY! OY! OY VAY! . . . ɢᴇVALT!
Oy, Jesus Christ [lit., "sweet little father (in heaven)"] *woe is me,*
oy, oy, oy vay, shee–it!

This is what the producer mentioned at the beginning of this book didn't want to know.

A man who has an ᴏᴏPʟᴏʏᴇ—an ejaculation—is said to shoot or shoot out. The verbs are

SHISN	OYSsʜɪsɴ
to shoot	*to shoot, fire, go off, explode*

A SHIS OYS IN GLEIKH ᴀROYS

A SHIS OYS IN GLEIKH ᴀROYS

Wham, bam, thank you, ma'am [lit., "a shot and straight out"].

Twelve Terms for Female Genitalia

As mentioned before, this is one topic that Yiddish would prefer to avoid, and there's almost no terminology for it that isn't clinical, euphemistic, or obscene. It's no wonder that *dortn*—"there"—is probably heard far more frequently, from women and men alike, than any of the terms below.

vᴀGEEɴᴇʜ (with a hard g)	MIᴛᴇʀsʜᴀʏᴅ
vagina	*vagina*
OYsᴇʜ MUᴋᴇᴍ	ERvᴇʜ
that place	*pudendum*

There isn't really much to say about these, except that *oyseh mukem,* the preferred rabbinic term also found in manuals of "family purity" directed to women, is basically a fancy Hebrew version of *dortn*—and *dortn* is much easier to say.

ZAKH	(YAIɴᴇʜ) MEIsᴇʜ	SHPEEL
thing	*(that) story, (that) matter*	*play, game*

Zakh—not to be confused with the reflexive pronoun—means "thing," and is probably the most benign of the three terms just listed. In this context, it's similar in both tone and meaning to the English *thing* or even *thang*. *(Yaineh) meiseh* is basically "that-matter-that-I-don't-have-to-tell-you-about (because you already know)," "her you-know-what"; it is, however, quite dirty, on a par, roughly speaking, with the English "snatch." It's the sort of thing you'd expect to see in the Yiddish edition of *Juggs* mentioned above.

Shpeel occupies a place analogous to that of *kazoo* in English, a good and neutral word suddenly turned to an agent of contempt. In 1928, when words of a certain type were hard to find in mainstream

English publications, Alexander Harkavy—in a dictionary published by the Hebrew Publishing Company in New York—defined *shpeel* in this sense as "cunt."

PEERGEH	KNISH	LOKH
pierogi	*knish*	*hole*

Peergeh and *knish* are vulgar but potentially affectionate terms; *knish*, at least, can be used by those who have one with the same aplomb as by those who don't. They're both comparable to the English "pussy," but—as befits a nation that sometimes expresses its joy through the creation and consumption of chopped-liver swans—with a culinary origin that makes them the obvious choices for idioms concerned with oral sex:

ZEE IZ AN ALTeh PEERGeh-FRESern

She's an old pierogi eater

is the Yiddish for "She's a carpet muncher from way back." If you describe a man as a PEERGEH-NASHer or, less commonly, a KNISH-FRESer, you're saying that he's predisposed to cunnilingus, a word that exists in Yiddish (KOONELINGoos) but is never used, probably because it sounds too much like *kooneh-laiml* (see page 146).

Knish seems to be a bit warmer than *peergeh*, and is one of the few such colloquialisms by which I've heard a woman refer to her own, unless she were deliberately talking "dirty." (The fairly common *SHMUNDEE*—an English-influenced version of the quite vulgar *SHMUNDEH*—was the girls' counterpart of young boys' *petsl* and *shmekl*, inoffensive kid versions of *pots* and *shmok*.) Indeed, *PEERGEH-MEKLer*, "pierogi broker," is slang for a pimp, and verbs that refer to nibbling, snacking, eating, and stuffing oneself are generally used when talking *about* such activities. In discussion leading to immediate performance, the preferred verb is *lekn*, "to lick." If you want your lover to do it, ask him or her to *lek* that *knish*.

If, however,

A FROY TIT OON POdeshkes MIT SHVARtseh ZOKN (IN EFsher A POOR
HOYkheh oopTSASN derTSEE)
*A woman puts on a garter belt and black stockings (and maybe a pair
of high heels, too),*

she might well command her lover to *es* her *peergeh*—it helps to
make things dirtier. *Fress* might be used in the heat of action—it's
the oral counterpart of "harder, faster," or "keep going, this is how
I like it."

You can avoid the whole problem by using *gaibm looshn,* the
idiom for French kissing that we saw in the section on necking. It
doesn't seem to make much difference *where* the tongue ends up.

There's one more food-based term that can't be ignored in this
context:

HOOmenTASH
hamentash,

a triangle-shaped piece of dough stuffed variously with poppy
seed, prunes, or walnuts that's eaten on Purim. Its shape and the
contrasting colors of the dough and the fillings have led to its being used as a Yiddish counterpart of "hair pie." *Hoomentash* is less
vulgar than *peergeh* or *knish,* and its festive associations lend it the
kind of jovial, even jaunty air that explains the smiles on the faces
of my relatives when my three-year-old daughter gave an im-
promptu performance of the Spice Girls' hit, "Stop," and, instead
of "I need somebody with a human touch," sang, "I need somebody with a hamentash."

At least she didn't ask for a Yule log.

9

Happiness and Pleasure

The fact that Yiddish is somewhat less forthcoming with positive emotions than most, if not all other languages, does not mean that it lacks the ability to convey feelings of happiness, pleasure, or satisfaction. It isn't the will to be happy that is absent, but the will to *talk* about being happy, the will to let anybody *know* that you're happy. The pervasive fear that opening your mouth could allow the forces of evil to ruin your life means that many of the terms that we're about to look at are used more often in the second and third person than in the first. Talking about happiness in Yiddish is like asking someone their age; the easiest way to do so is to pack all the necessary demon repellents, carefully worded good wishes and other protective impedimenta into a single *Jeopardy*-like question that already contains ninety percent of the answer. We saw a long time ago that the easiest way to get an unambiguous statement of age out of a certain type of Yiddish-speaker is to ask:

VEE ALT IZ DER YID, BIZ HINᴅᴇʀᴛ IN TSVONᴛsɪᴋ
How old is the Jew [i.e., you], may he live to 120?

Outside of petrified conventional phrases that are used strictly for the sake of form—"Nice to meet you," for example—most expressions of happiness, pleasure, or satisfaction are uttered on behalf of the person experiencing the emotion by the person who is asking about it. For example:

SAUL BELLOW'S FATHER: MEIN ZEEN HOT NEKHTN
ɢᴇKROGN DEE NOʙᴇʟ-PRAIMʏᴇʜ
My son won the Nobel Prize yesterday.

ISAAC BASHEVIS SINGER: MAZL TOV, IKH BIN ZIkher AZ EER
SHEPT FEEL NAkhes
Mazl tov, I'm sure that it's giving you a great deal of pleasure.

SAUL BELLOW'S FATHER: *[Smiles, beams and nods]:* MMMM . . .
Mmmm . . .

Note that the party who is happy never mentions happiness. He or she sticks to facts, descriptions of past events that can no longer be altered. It's the interlocutor who introduces emotion because the demons, as well as the guys with evil eyes, need direct confirmation if they're to have any dominion at all—a confirmation denied them by the subjunctive character of the phrase "I'm sure" and Bellow *père's* response of "Mmmm . . . ," which have put them out of business—at least for the moment.

Why are Jews so prominent in journalism and the law? Yiddish taught us all how to ask the right questions.

Yiddish has a number of words for pleasure:

FARGeNEEGN   TEINeg   HANOOeh

can all be defined as "pleasure" or "delight," but each has its own range of uses. *Fargeneegn* is the most basic word for pleasure, colorless enough to cover anything from conventional pleasantries to genuine enjoyment:

A FARGeNEEGN TSE ZEIN DOO
A pleasure to be here, nice to be here

IKH VEL KIMen MIT GROYS FARGeNEEGN
I'll be delighted to attend

DOOS FARGeNEEGN FIN FARBRENGen MIT IM
the pleasure of his company [lit., "the pleasure of spending
time with him"].

246

One of the great off-color songs in the modern Yiddish reper-
toire is based on a risqué parody of an old radio commercial for a
clothing store. Said to have been originated (though never
recorded) by Red Buttons, it opens with:

> JOE AND PAUL'S A FARGeNEEGN,
> *Joe and Paul's, it's a pleasure,*

> JOE AND PAUL'S MEH KEN A BARGain KREEGN
> *Joe and Paul's, you can get a bargain.*

The *fargeneegn* was borrowed from the original commercial, and is
no more meaningful than "pleasure" would have been in English.
"Joe and Paul's [it's] a pleasure"; all it really says is that you won't
actively regret having dropped into Joe and Paul's to pick up a suit.
What's really important, in both the original commercial and the
quotation above (from the Barton Brothers' 1947 recording), is
that *fargeneegn* rhymes with *kreegn*.

Teineg is more precise than *fargeneegn* and refers only to genuine, active enjoyment:

> MEH KLEIBT TEINeg FIN ZITSN IN SHVITS
> *People take pleasure/delight in sitting in a steam bath.*

Simple lack of chagrin isn't enough; *a teineg* involves physical or
emotional sensations that are slightly out of the ordinary, pleasur-
able enough for you to want to repeat them.

The source of pleasure is described as a *teineg;* the verb to use if
you're experiencing the feeling is *kleibm,* "to gather, collect":

> IKH KLEIB TEINeg FIN SHPEELN peeAneh
> *I really enjoy playing the piano.*

More common than *teineg, hanooeh* is used in the virtually indispensable idiom

HₐNOOₑH HOBM

to enjoy, have fun,

which is the sort of thing that you say or hear every day:

HOST HₐNOOₑH GₑHAT FINₑM KₒNTSERT?

Did you enjoy the concert?

HOST HₐNOOₑH GₑHAT?

Did you have fun? Enjoy yourself? Have a good time?

Authors of Yiddish books will often inscribe copies of their work with

HOT HₐNOOₑH

Enjoy.

In describing anything that affords *hanooeh,* you can also use the closely related verb

NAIₙₑₕ ZEIN

to benefit from, enjoy, profit from, partake of:

DEE FₐrAYₙᵢₖₜₑₕ SHTATN ZEₙₑₙ NAIₙₑₕ FIN ZAYₑr NOOₑₙₜₖₑᵢₜ

TSE KₐNAdₑₕ

The U.S.A. benefits from its closeness to Canada

ER HOT NAIₙₑₕ GₑVAIN FIN EER ARbₑₜ

He profited from/enjoyed the fruits of her labors.

Far more common than any of the words that we've just looked at,

ₜₛₑFREEDN

pleased, satisfied, happy, glad, content

is used ironically as often as not.

ₜₛₑFREEDN?

Happy?

or

BIST ᴛꜱᴇFREEDN?

You happy?

usually means either: "Nice going. You didn't listen and now you've wrecked it" (whether it's a toy, a relationship, or your life), or, "*Nu,* after the incredible fuss that you kicked up to get things your own way, are you really any happier? Was it worth the effort and the complete loss of my esteem?"

More positively, if you like the way things are going or think that something is working out well, you can use *tsefreedn* with no ironic overtones at all:

IKH BIN ᴛꜱᴇFREEDN VOOS DEE BIST DOO MIT INDZ

I'm happy that you're here with us

ZEE IZ ᴛꜱᴇFREEDN MIT DEE NEIʏᴇʜ OONɢᴇSHTELᴛᴇʜ

She's happy with the new employees.

Had Señor Wences performed in Yiddish, he'd have asked Pedro, the puppet head inside the wooden box,

ᴛꜱᴇFREEDN?

All right? [lit., "happy?"]

and the puppet would have answered with

ᴛꜱᴇFREEDN

S'all right.

Satisfaction of urges or desires is expressed through the verb

ᴛꜱᴇFREEDN SHTELN

to satisfy, accommodate, gratify.

"I can't get no satisfaction" would come out as

GOORɴɪsʜᴛ SHTELT MIKH NISHT ᴛsᴇFREEDN

Nothing satisfies me.

Tsefreedn shteln will be a staple of customer service departments, once they start to run such departments in Yiddish:

ʀᴀBOYsᴇɪ, MIR KENᴇɴ ZAY NISHT ᴛsᴇFREEDN SHTELN,

NOR ꜰᴀʀᴘᴀMAIʟᴇᴋʜɴ

Gentlemen, we cannot satisfy them, only slow them down.

Nakhes, often spelled "nachos" in English, is probably the best-known of all Yiddish words having to do with pleasure. If a phrase like

NAᴋʜᴇs FIN KINᴅᴇʀ

pleasure that you get from your children

hasn't yet entered English, it isn't for want of trying. *Nakhes* pops up often enough on TV and in movies to suggest that even people who keep Christmas are familiar with it. It means "delight, pleasure," but it means so much more than "delight" or "pleasure." Uriel Weinreich glosses it as "(spiritual) pleasure," by which he means only that you can't get any *nakhes* from a body rub (though the rub itself can be a *mekheiyeh*). The pleasure to which *nakhes* refers is intangible, unquantifiable; it takes place in the mind, rather than the body, and is entirely a matter of disposition or point of view. A graduation ceremony means nothing to you until a child of yours is one of the graduates.

You can

KLEIBM NAᴋʜᴇs

gather, collect nakhes,

just as you do with *teineg.* More commonly, though, a person is said to

SHEPN NAkhes

to draw/ladle up nakhes

as if it were water coming out of a well or air going into your lungs:

MEH SHEPT LIFT

You draw breath [lit., "air"]

in Yiddish in exactly the same way as you seek satisfaction. And it's a lot easier to get air, a fact made all the more clear when we take a look at what *nakhes* really means. It's a Hebrew word that starts out meaning "peace, quiet, rest," as in the book of Ecclesiastes:

> Better a handful of quietness [*nakhes*] than two hands full of toil
> and a striving after wind (4:6).
> The words of the wise heard in quiet [*nakhes*] are better than
> the shouting of a ruler among fools (9:17).

Yiddish identifies the deepest, most soulful pleasure with listening, with keeping quiet, with hearing the voices of others, and with being left alone. *Nakhes,* then, is a psychic vacation, a departure from the usual conditions of life, and its source is never within; you've got to find it outside, you have to scoop it up and draw it to yourself from wherever it might abide, knowing all the while that it's a wasting resource and that there's no guarantee of a refill. A rest is very nice, but naptime can't last forever.

Such a view of the nature of happiness leads to some unusual ways of describing it:

MEH VERT GRUB FIN NAkhes

You get fat with pleasure

MEH VERT BRAYter VEE LENger

You swell up with pride [lit., "become as wide as you are tall"].

Once you've got it, you do your best never to let it go; it isn't anything that you're about to reveal in public. It's hard enough to hold onto it as it is, God help you if you're going to put it out there where some S.O.B. can come by and grab it. Remember the education from page 3, the one that can't be taken away from you? *Nakhes,* handled right, is the emotional counterpart of that college degree. Holding it in is no more selfish or niggardly than accepting money to practice medicine or locking your door at night; it's a matter of simple common sense.

This idea of holding it in—think of it as the emotional tantra of Ashkenazi Judaism (and remember that "tantra" could just as well be the plural of "tantrum")—is also present in another well-known term for enjoying oneself. *Kveln,* which often comes up in English as, "I'm *kvelling,*" that is, "I'm delighted; I'm more than delighted, I'm positively reveling in pleasure and pride," has a fundamental meaning of "to flow, spring, gush." But in this case, whatever is in motion is not coming out. That's why people have to tell you that they're *kvelling* (something that can happen in English, but not in real Yiddish). They might be slightly flushed with pleasure, but that light dusting of *nakhes* on the surface of the skin is all that's allowed out.

Kveln also conveys a sense of expansion, of swelling. The verb is usually used in a complemented form, OONKVELN, in which the *oon*-prefix gives *kveln* an explicit sense of swelling up:

ER KVELT OON FIN ZEIneh KINder
His children make him beam with joy,

means that you can see him swelling up with pride and pleasure until he's just this side of bursting—and the Yiddish for "to burst" is *platsn,* as in the semi-English, "I almost *platsed,*" (sometimes spelled *plotzed*) i.e., was shocked or upset to the point of bursting.

The difference between joy and dismay seems to be that no one has ever had so much *nakhes* as to have burst for *kvelling*.

Happy people can be described as

FRAYlekh   LIStik

merry, cheerful, joyful   *cheerful, merry.*

They're

MOOleh-SIMkheh

full of joy, delighted,

because things are an absolute

meKHEIyeh

delight, pleasure.

Mekheiyeh comes from the Hebrew and is actually short for *mekheiyeh* neFOOshes, "restoring people to life, revivifying." It works particularly well in a swimming pool, steam bath, or an air-conditioned building when it's scorchingly hot outside:

OY, IZ DOOS A meKHEIyeh

Oy, it's like I'm back from the dead.

And there you have it, the ultimate expression of Yiddish joy: I almost forgot I'm alive.

Fin—from, of, 27

FINger (-), der—finger, toe, 86, 178

FINster—dark, 21, 162

FLANken, dee (*plu.*)—flank steak, 67

FLAYshik—of meat; makhn zakh FLAYshik—to have a drink; to get high; to start a business, 60–62, 221

FLIRteven—to flirt, 219

Flokn (s), der—pole, club, 151

Floy (flay), der—flea, 137

Fnyeh—indicative of a lack of enthusiasm, 111, 112

Folk (FELker), doos—people, nation, 166, 167

Foorn (iz geFOORN)—to go (by vehicle), 164

FOORshteln (hot FOORgeshtelt)—to present, 20

Foorts (ferts), der—fart, 43, 154, 187

FOOter (s), der—father, 79–80

foTO-apaRAT (n), der—camera, 178

Foyl—lazy, rotten, 228

FRAIG-NISHT/NISHtseh (s), der/dee—your "adult" child's live-in lover, 217

Fraign (hot geFRAIGT)—to ask, 19, 216, 233

frantseVAteh—syphilitic; foul, 192

Frantsn, dee (*plu.*)—syphilis, 191, 192

FRAYen zakh (hot zakh geFRAYT)—to be glad, 90

FRAYlekh—merry, cheerful, 29, 253

FREEer—before, earlier, 190

FREEling (en), der—spring (season), 168

FREEshtik (n), der—breakfast, 63

Fresn (hot geFREST)—to gorge oneself, eat like a pig, 54

Froy (en), dee—woman, wife; Mrs., 20, 40, 77, 217, 221–22, 244, 256, 258

Frum—pious, religious (used here as an English word; it'd be *frim* in this book's Yiddish), 10

GAInets (n), der—yawn, 185, 223

GAInetsn (hot geGAInetst)—to yawn, 185

Gal, dee—gall, bile, 55, 177

Gandz (gendz), dee—goose, 67, 215

GAnef (gaNOvim)—thief, rascal, 131, 154

Gants—whole, entire; in gantsn—completely, 15, 18, 54, 91, 95, 128, 140, 182, 185, 196, 198, 224, 227

Gartl (en), der—belt, 118, 194

GAZlen (gazLONim), der—bandit, robber, 154

GDIleh (s), dee—glory; something worth bragging about; big deal, 119, 120

geDAIrem, dee (*plu.*)—intestines, bowels, 177

geDILD, doos—patience, 144

geDOYlim, dee (*plu.*)—defecation, 188

geFAR (n), dee—danger, 113

geFELN (iz geFELN)—to please; es geFELT meer—I like it, 20, 31, 196, 221

geFILT—stuffed, 67

geFInen (hot geFINen)—to find, 43, 204, 218

geHAKT—chopped, cut up, 67, 204, 218

geHARget—killed, 159, 260

Gel—yellow, 191

geLENK (en), doos—wrist, ankle, 172

GELzukht, dee—jaundice, 190

geNIG—enough, 82, 168–69, 202, 213

geRIKHT (n), doos—course (of meal), dish, 53, 215

Gern—gladly, happily, willingly, 93, 201

geROOTN—successful; clever and attractive, 84–85, 136

geSHEFT (n), doos—business, 130

geSHLIFN—smooth, glib, polished, 10

geSHVEER (n), doos—abscess, 164

geTRIKNteh FLOYmen, dee (*plu.*)—prunes, 64

geTSAITLT—on a list, 39

Getsh (es), der—idol, idiot, 148

geVALdik—great, powerful, fantastic, 50, 127

geVALT (geVALDN), dee—force, violence, 46, 48, 49, 50, 241

geVALT (geVALDN), der—scream, hue and cry; gevalt!—help!, 48–50

geVInen (hot geVInen)—to win, 119

geZES (n), doos—seat, buttocks, 175, 176

geZINT—healthy, well; zei geZINT—good-bye, 16, 17, 77, 162, 180, 185

geZINterhayt—in good health, 17, 180

GILden—golden, of gold; GILdeneh OOder—hemorrhoids, 194

Gilgl (gilGIlim), der—reincarnation; transformation; evil spirit, 89

Git—good, 4, 13, 14–15, 16, 18, 23, 81, 138, 181

Glaitn (hot geGLAIT)—to pet, stroke, caress, 224

Glaybm (hot geGLAYBT)—to believe, 130, 259

Gleikh—right away; straight, 242

Glist, der—desire, lust, 215

Glitshn zakh (hot zakh geGLITSHT)—to slip; to skate, 22

Glomp (n), der—stalk or stem of cabbage or lettuce; idiot, 151

Glooz (GLAIzer), doos—glass, 53, 92

Gold—gold, 48

GOOen (geOYnim), der—genius, 150

Goopl (en), der—fork, 53

Goor—totally, quite, extremely, completely, 41, 95

GOORnisht—nothing, 203, 250

Got (GEter), der—god, 80, 103

got-ELF—good afternoon, 13

GOYlem (goyLOmim/GOYlems), der—golem, 146, 161–62

GRAIber—comparative of *grub*, 54

Grais (n), dee—size, 137

Green—green, 55

GREger (s), der—noisemaker used on Purim; penis, 233

Greps (n), der—belch, eructation, 185, 207

Grepsn (hot geGREPST)—to burp, 54

Gribl (akh), doos—shallow pit or hole in ground, 96

grobYAN (en), der—uncouth jerk, 155

Groys—big, great, 23, 246, 257, 258

Grub—fat, coarse, obscene, lewd, 213, 220, 251

GVEEres, dee (*plu.*)—eightieth birthday, 42, 44

Hakn (hot geHAKT)—to chop, knock, bang, 202–3

Haldz (HELdzer), der—neck, throat, 172

Haldzn zakh (hot zakh geHALDZT)—to embrace, 225, 227

haliBOOT (n), der—halibut, 67

Haltn (hot geHALTN)—to hold, think, contain, keep, 23, 98, 116, 216

Ham, der—(*baby talk*) food; (*dim.*) HAmenyoo; HAmen—to eat, 108

haNOOeh (s), dee—pleasure, enjoyment; haNOOeh hobm—to enjoy, 246, 247–48

Hant (hent), dee—hand, 21, 112, 216

Hant-geLENK (en)—wrist, 172

Harb—strong, harsh, difficult, 10

HARgenen (hot geHARget)—to kill, 159, 167, 260

Harts (HERtser), doos—heart, 61, 177, 178

HARTSreisenish (n), doos—heartbreak, 218

HARTSvaytik (n), der—heartbreak, 218

Hays—hot, 21, 22, 138

Haysn (hot geHAYSN)—to be called, named; to order, 20

HEEger/HEEgeh—local, from here; American-born, 141

Heen (HEEner), dee—chicken, hen, 67, 119

HEFker—ownerless, 66

Heint—today, 20, 31, 42, 89, 93, 107, 119, 126, 135, 167, 169

HEIteh (s), dee—(*baby talk*) walk; gayn HEIteh—to take a walk, 108

HEKHsher (hekhSHAIrim), der—rabbinical seal of approval, 57–59

Hekht (–), der—pike (fish); sucker, sap, 67